THE SEVEN PATHS
TO SUCCESS

A Behind the Scenes Look at Success
& Getting Everything You Want

AINSLEY ALLEN

THE SEVEN PATHS TO SUCCESS

A Behind the Scenes Look at Success
& Getting Everything You Want

Rachel Bandara
Renee "The Bare Boss" Gambino
Mike Gillette
Renée Jones
Ana Rosenberg
Nicole "RapWithNic" Welch
David C. Williams

TABLE OF CONTENTS

"A coach is someone who tells you what you don't want to hear, who has you see what you don't want to see, so that you can be who you have always known you could be." Tom Landry.

Considered one of the greatest football coaches of all time, NFL great Tom Landry offered his players more than simple direction. He inspired them to be a better version of themselves, which is in essence what makes a great coach.

Tom Landry's contributions to the game of football go above and beyond simple wins and losses, although those are substantial. Landry's innovative way of playing the game actually is what made him such as success. For example, during Landry's reign as the coach of America's team--the Dallas Cowboys--he and his staff became the very first to computerize the process of scouting, game planning and preparation. He also reintroduced the shotgun formation on offense and created the 4-3 defense, which are still staples of pro football. His success was a combination of innovation in the game of football and a committed, albeit distanced relationship with his players.

Landry's achievements as a coach in turn led to the success of countless players and even other coaches whom he had a hand in shaping. Landry wasn't a touchy feely type of guy, yet he made each and every player and coach he worked with more successful because of his commitment to innovation and excellence.

In addition to Tom Landry, there are a host of other coaches in sports, business and life who have had a huge impact on the achievements of those whom they inspired, trained and directed. In fact, there are many professionals who owe a portion, if not most of, their success in business, sports or life to their coaches.

Successful People Who Found
Worth in Great Coaching

Bob Nardelli: Nardelli became the CEO of the home improvement merchandising giant Home Depot in 2000 and promptly began an overhaul. The changes he made eliminated various divisions and streamlined the company's operations. The most effective changes he made were to automate the inventory systems and centralize the supply orders to the Atlanta headquarters. The end result of his various improvements was an increase in Home Depot's competitive position. Not to mention the fact that during his reign, he doubled the chain's sales. Nardelli is credited with Home Depot's success during his time of leadership for good reason. Therefore, his take on leadership and business can most certainly be trusted. The following is a statement he made pertaining to the subject:

"I absolutely believe that people, unless coached, never reach their maximum capabilities." Bod Nardelli

Tanya Clemens: Due to her role as the Vice President of Global Executive & Organizational Development for the IBM Corporation, which is short for International Business Machines Corporation, Tanya Clemens knows what she is talking about in regards to leadership and success. IBM employs over 10,000 people and currently boasts over $5 billion in revenues; ergo, the company in which Tanya Clemens serves is prosperous to say the least. Therefore, her findings on the role of coaching in regards to business are worth noting:

"We have done lots of research over the past three years, and we have found that leaders who have the best coaching skills have better business results." Tanya Clemons.

This statement by Clemons simply reiterates the importance of coaching in all facets of a business. For example, its presence is highly valuable in terms of helping CEOs achieve greater success in part by making them better leaders themselves, and it is also valuable in the lower ranks of the company.

Coaching is Worth the Investment

Coaching of any kind, be it life coaching, business coaching or fitness coaching is an investment in the betterment of life and overall health. Therefore, instead of considering it an expense, look at it as an investment toward greater general well being. The following is a breakdown of a few popular types of coaching and why they are well worth the investment.

Life Coaching

Life coaching is basically employing a coach who will help individuals in their personal development. It is different than counseling or therapy. Instead of just talking about feelings and emotions, although that can be part of it, a life coach will help define personal projects or help an individual transition in regards to various changes in their personal life. In short, it helps them make their life what they want it to be.

Henry David Thoreau once said, *"Go confidently in the direction of your dreams! Live the life you've imagined. As you simplify your life, the laws of the universe will be simpler."*

In essence, without even knowing of its existence, Thoreau sums up what life coaching is all about through his quote. The following are a few additional benefits of life coaching or personal development.

Makes You Self-Aware – Understand this doesn't mean that life coaching will make an individual selfish, just that they will begin to see who they really are. What are their values? What is their purpose and what goals do they want to pursue? After all, no one can ever achieve their own dreams when they are busy working towards others' ideals.

Gives a Definite Sense of Direction – After raising the self-awareness level, individuals who have invested in coaching will see things in their life much clearer. This enables them to set their direction.

Improves Your Effectiveness and Focus – Once a direction and purpose is clearly defined, individuals are able to focus more on those goals. This in turn increases their effectiveness substantially. Remember, a blind squirrel will find a nut every now and then, but one with vision fulfills his goal much more frequently.

Once a life coach helps someone focus on their goals, better define them and helps them learn how to dream for themselves, their whole mindset changes. This means that they are now ultra-focused.

Fitness or Wellness Coaching

Another type of coaching is fitness coaching or personal training, which is often referred today as simply wellness coaching. This is a coach who works with individuals one-on-one to develop a plan for fitness and emotional well-being. If individuals are easily distracted at the gym or lack the motivation to remain faithful to a workout, a wellness coach is an ideal investment. This person will walk alongside them, literally, as they transform both their inner and outer beings simultaneously. Although this type of specific wellness coaching is still in the newer side of the field, some doctors are even catching on to the benefits of this type of program and recommending it for their patients. Wellness coaching is really the combination of fitness coaching with a counselor for an inner and outer transformation. The following are just a few of the many benefits that can be derived from wellness or fitness coaching

Personalized Goal Setting – A coach will work to define what a person's health goals are and then create a plan to achieve that goal.

Accountability – More than anything else, wellness coaching is most beneficial for the simple fact that it gives accountability. Individuals will have someone checking up on them, which will encourage them to show up at the gym or to turn down that extra piece of cake.

Educates You – A wellness coach will also educate those they are working with on how to better their life, giving them the tools to make their own life better.

Business Coaching

"Business coaching is attracting America's top CEOs because; put simply, business coaching works. In fact, when asked for a conservative estimate of monetary payoff from the coaching they got...managers described average returns of more than $100,000, or about six times what the coaching had cost their companies." FORTUNE Magazine.

As this statement exemplifies, the investment in a business coach yields a greater return by far than any money spent on hiring the coach in the first place. Therefore, from a dollars and cents perspective, it just makes sense.

Why Business Coaches are Necessary - According to the Harvard Business Review, two out of every five new CEOs fail within their first 18 months on the job. The reason they fail has nothing to do with their knowledge, experience or competence. Instead, it seems the impetus behind the failure is their inability to lead effectively.

Case in point, research shows that 82% of newly appointed leaders fail simply because of their inability to build partnerships with their peers and subordinates. In other words, they cannot lead or encourage others to lead. Thankfully, those leaders who garner the help of a business coach are more prepared for this aspect of their new role and thus are more likely to succeed.

Role of Business Coach – The role of the business coach is best described as a person who comes alongside the leaders in a company and makes them more effective. They encourage innovative thinking and inspire those they direct to be the very best version of themselves.

Just as sports coaches, like coach Landry mentioned above, inspire their players to give it their all each and every time they suit up, business, wellness and life coaches encourage individuals to strive for a better version of their best effort. They do this by limiting distractions, setting healthy boundaries, helping leaders to define workable goals and encouraging them to understand the benefits and the strategies behind delegation, among many other contributions. Therefore, the role of coach is vastly important and should be considered invaluable for anyone who wishes to succeed in business or in life.

Success

Success can be defined in any number of ways. Some people measure success in terms of how much money or how many things they can accumulate over a lifetime. Others have a less materialistic interpretation of the word and equate the completion of any task or meeting of any goal to mean success. Still others believe success is simply being able to achieve happiness in their life. In our journey through life we all encounter difficult situations that can become obstacles to success. Overcoming obstacles is a key to success.

Successful people rarely do it alone. To paraphrase an old, but still relevant truth, "behind every successful man or woman is another individual or group of individuals". It may be your spouse, business partner, doctor, or good friend who is there when you need them the most. A motivational speaker can make you think in an entirely different way that will steer you in the right direction to achieve your dreams. Whether you are trying to build stronger relationships or improve your health, there is someone who will help you achieve your goal. To be sure, if you want to succeed in business, having people you can trust and count on to be on your side will help guide you forward. History teaches us that the most successful people do not do it alone.

It is one thing to make it to the top and an entirely different thing to stay there. Success can be fleeting but it can also be something that will stay with you throughout your life. In a team sport like football, the quarterback may get all the glory for winning the Super Bowl but credit for his success has to be shared with his team and coaches. Tom Brady of the New England Patriots is a superstar, but without protection from his offensive line along with the guidance and feedback form his coach, he would struggle to complete a pass.

Staying at the top, whether it is in sports, business, or anything else, may be more difficult than getting there. Sustaining the success you have achieved is tough to do alone. Surrounding yourself with experts, who have certain skills that you may not possess, is crucial in almost any business.

The Seven Paths of Success contains powerful and fascinating conversations with seven passionate coaches who have played such an influential role in the success of so many others. As you read their insightful stories and learn from their experiences remember, just one small tip from any of these dedicated and driven individuals could be just the spark that turns your life around and walks you down the path to success you are seeking.

A Fresh Start in Life May Be the Best Thing to Happen to You

A fresh start in life is rarely carefully planned out. Rather, they tend to be thrust upon you when you least expect it. Furthermore, fresh starts are hardly ever the result of a positive or happy experience. Think job loss or divorce.

In this interview, Rachel Bandara reveals how she personally turned a fresh start into the best thing that ever happened to her – and how she now helps other women do the same – whether it's in a career, business, image, relationships or life in general.

She helps them develop an empowering, fulfilling and authentic lifestyle that enables them to reach the potential that they know they are capable of, even if they feel that change is impossible.

Many women actually end up finding that the negative experience that thrust them into a fresh start may lead them into directions they never even conceived they would want to go, with startling and wonderful results.

Conversation with Rachel Bandara

Let's start exploring what the term Fresh Start means. I think to a lot of people a Fresh Start usually occurs as the result of something that has happened unexpectedly and is probably not a positive or happy experience.

Have you found that a fresh start is something people choose to undertake, or is it something that they're thrown into because circumstances have changed drastically in their lives?

Rachel Bandara: I think you're absolutely right. Most people do get thrown into it and it can be quite unexpected. There may be a very small portion that might choose to say, "I'm doing well but I need to do a bit better." But, most of my clientele are people who got thrown into a situation and they are in desperate need of a fresh start.

What are some examples of the situations that create that need for a Fresh Start? Are these circumstances your clients just didn't see coming?

Rachel Bandara: Let's take divorce for example. You are going through life and everything's going well – or you think it's going well – and then the divorce comes. Or, you get laid off from a job that you took a lot of pride in and put a lot of effort into.

When these things happen, it brings with it such a huge impact on your personal life. Some of us may not admit it, but the impact that it carries is quite significant.

What people find when they're in these situations is that they lose their identity. Their very identity about who they are, what they stand for, and their purpose in their life.

All of those get thrown out the window and they feel lost and helpless, and it's a terrible place to be.

That's a really important point you make. On the surface one might think, "Well, they're going through a divorce." The solution is to find another relationship or fix the relationship that they were in. Or, if they lost a job, the solution is to find another job or find another source of income.

But you just mentioned how tightly a job or relationship is tied to someone's identity. When people get divorced, it's not only that they're out of a relationship, now they're no longer Mr. or Mrs. So-and-so.

When someone loses a job, it's not just about loss of income. They're no longer Director of This or Chief of That. People have grown up in a society where that's what you identify with.

Compared to replacing income or finding a new relationship how important and just how much value do people place on that identity?

Rachel Bandara: If people have been doing the same job for a long time, or if they have been in a relationship for a long time, they start attaching their identity to that. "I'm someone's wife," or "I do this." If they go to a party, they might introduce themselves as "I'm the Director of Such-and-such Company."

Their whole identity then starts getting built and strengthened based on the role they play.

Now, when circumstances happen that force them out of where they are, that's a mighty uncomfortable situation. They no longer have the context to define themselves. When they are left like that, they get what I call "stripped down bare." You get stripped naked again to the absolute quintessential you – who you are.

Now, people have to often try and rediscover themselves when they lose their identity. It's a very challenging situation, but the good news about that is it's actually amazing when people do recover their identities. It's absolutely possible and I have seen hundreds of people do it.

In the beginning it can be very overwhelming for the people you help. When they're stripped of that identity, besides being at a loss of what to call themselves, have you found a great deal of the confidence that they may have carried in life was also tied to that identity?

Rachel Bandara: Yes. Confidence is a huge thing. When there's a lot of change happening in people's lives, confidence seems to be one of the first things that takes a beating whether in a relationship situation or job situation.

Once your confidence takes a dive, then you start questioning your identity and who you are and what you stand for. And, yes, when clients come to me, in that first session, it's very much an overwhelmed, "Oh, my gosh! I don't know what to do and where to go from here."

Or "I've been confident for a long time. And now, I know I need to make a change but I have no idea where to start."

That's where the fresh start comes in.

When someone is overwhelmed by these circumstances, perhaps even in a state of panic, what needs to happen for them to be able to begin to rebuild and say "Okay, the fresh start – this is where we start changing things"?

Rachel Bandara: I think when people are going through change or are in a place of needing a fresh start, they don't usually see what they need to do, when they are in that state of overwhelm.

When you're in that position, it's very difficult for someone to just say, "This is what you need to do. Do these five steps. Take it home and do that and you'll be fine." It doesn't quite work like that. That's because if they're questioning their very identity on a day-to-day basis, that needs to be dealt with first.

When I say dealt with, it means helping to establish who you are. Who your authentic self is. Maybe the job or the role that you were playing was not exactly the right fit for you. So, it could be a blessing in disguise, this situation that you're in.

Most of my clients would find it difficult to believe this in the beginning, but then they work through it and then they start finding those hidden gems that they had inside, that they hadn't paid attention to. For example, they could be a really gifted writer but they put that aside to maybe become a housewife or maybe to become a business analyst or whatever role that they've chosen in life.

That means that in certain situations, my clients discover that there's another part of me and there are other gifts inside of me that I can discover.

All of a sudden, they start to see possibilities. And that's exciting.

What you're talking about is so incredibly important and I think a part of why you're so good at what you do.

You have really put a spotlight on the concept and value of "Being Authentic" and helping your clients figure out if the identity they have been attached to for so long has just been a role that they've been playing in order to conform, rather than living as who they really are.

There are a lot of people who give up on dreams in a part of their life in order to do what they think they are supposed to do or be the person the think they're supposed to be.

A fresh start, from your methods, is not just about getting back on track. You say, "No, let's take this and really make it fresh. Let's discover who you are really meant to be. Let's discover what you are really meant to do, which may not be getting back on that same path. You may find a completely different path."

Give some examples where people were playing that role for so long, but then were able to rediscover a different authentic self that they were really meant to be.

Rachel Bandara: That's my story right there because I'm a very creative person and always have been. However, I started working in a management role that I thought was very good for me, and it had taught me some immense life skills. No, don't get me wrong, I absolutely loved the job that I was in.

However, once you're in something for too long, you start to believe that that's where you're meant to be. Just like my clients, until I was forced into a situation where I had to question everything about what I stood for. I didn't realize I had pushed away my own creativity, my own authentic self just so I could fit into a role.

It's amazing. It's so common for people to fit into a role because society expects them to or because their background reinforces their beliefs that they should do this or that. There are millions of reasons why they would choose to do that.

When people get forced into a corner, they all of a sudden start questioning and looking at things with a fresh set of eyes. You start realizing what you may have pushed away. And, again, that may be a whole career or a whole different path that you were meant to walk in, in the first place.

And that was how it was for me with coaching. My goodness, it feels so right now!

One of my clients, a lovely lady from Melbourne, was feeling very large and self-conscious when she came to me.

She was such a beautiful lady, and when she came to me, she said, "Look. Over the years, I've put on so much weight because every year I kept getting looked over for promotions at work and people just wouldn't give me the time of day because I was a little bit chubby."

Over the years, it reinforced her negative beliefs. She just kept eating more, not exercising, getting into a bit of depression and it's just a vicious cycle that you get stuck in.

When she came to me, she was in tears. She was saying, "Look. I have been stuck in the same position at work and I just can't get ahead. And I've come to this point where I look at myself and say, "Oh, my gosh. Who am I and what am I doing?"

I worked with her for a couple of sessions and she sent me an email saying, "Rachel, you won't believe it. I have started going to the gym and I have lost a little bit of weight. I have started dressing up a bit more professionally. Looking after myself. And also, I'm getting considered for a promotion."

This is a lady who had been overlooked for a promotion for the last seven or eight years. All of a sudden, after a couple of sessions, her perspective and her approach in life changed. She started believing and tapping into some of that authentic self of who she is.

Other people started sensing that, too. So yes, there are many stories like that.

It really is incredible. When they reach this point thinking, "I've got to figure out a way to get back." And what you're able to do is say, "Let's hold off. Maybe back isn't where you need to be."

When you talk about that being the exciting part, I can't imagine when that actually hits someone and they understand the concept that they may not be going back. Is this where they determine that maybe this divorce or this job loss was actually a good thing? Maybe this is the best thing that could have ever happened?

Do you see that this is a point where they maybe start recognizing this as something good or just tremendously beneficial to them, versus being the tragedy that they thought it was?

Rachel Bandara: Absolutely. And I can't even begin to describe how happy I feel when I see this point happening for a client when they see they don't have to go back.

When people come to me, they think that they're coming to do the program, to do the sessions so that they can get back to their relationship or the job or to whatever they were doing before, and just do better at that.

When you start working on finding out your authentic self and starting at that very bottom level and then working your way up from that – then people start to realize, "Oh, my goodness. I don't need to go back. I don't need to go back to a job that I only mildly like or I might actually hate, even though it's making me good money. I don't need to go back to this relationship. I have all these other possibilities in my business."

It's that point of realization when they look into themselves and see, "Oh, my goodness. My life has been narrowly focused on a certain part and that was what I thought was expected of me."

When they come to that realization, the freedom that they find when they realize I don't need that. Actually, I'm going to do something new. I feel empowered to do it because it seems so right with my authentic self and who I am.

All of a sudden, they're finding all this amazing courage. All these amazing coincidences in their lives and it's like everything's starting to fall into place. And when a client gets into that place, you can't stop them. They're off.

I can't even imagine how truly rewarding that is for you, witnessing the moment they realize that their confidence is something that was not attached to their previous identity, but rather attached to them, when they realize that they're able to be something more than what they thought. You had another powerful word for it – courage.

Do you find that the discovery of this all of a sudden brings up or generates more courage than they may have recognized that they had in a long time?

Rachel Bandara: The amount of courage that comes through from people at this point is absolutely life changing. Obviously, this is why I'm doing this coaching. This is why I do the programs with my clients.

All of a sudden, they dig deep inside themselves and find this massive wealth of courage that they never even knew existed. They are empowered to do whatever they want.

You talked about confidence, and I think I should really mention that because people attach a lot of confidence into the different roles that they play. I found this a lot in my corporate life, in the commercial experiences I've had.

I've seen this a lot where people come to work and they're completely different to how they are outside. It's almost like this massive role that they put on, a persona they put on to be at work. They start attaching confidence to that. They're no longer comfortable being their authentic self.

So what a massive change causes people to do is if their confidence has fallen apart, and that confidence was attached to a certain role, they start to look back into where their confidence should be attached to in the first place, which is their authentic self.

When your confidence is attached to that, you'll find that no crisis, no tragedy, no change in circumstances can really shake you because it's attached to who you are – not some kind of role that you're supposed to play.

That's extremely powerful.

We've been talking on a conceptual level, and I know that one of the things that you see a lot are people that have gotten this conceptual piece from self-help seminars or programs and that's kind of where it ends.

It seems this can do more damage than it does good because when just that conceptual piece doesn't work, they feel like they've failed. This won't work for them.

Let's talk about the tactical side of this; because you incorporate creative and holistic strategies along what some might view as being more clinical exercises such using data and information from traditional tools, like the Myers-Briggs Test.

Do you find that the data that is provided by some of these more traditional tools, such as Myers-Briggs, give you some really solid information that you're able to use to start discovering whether some-

one may not need to go back to whatever they were doing and may, in fact, need to discover what they were really meant to do?

Rachel Bandara: Absolutely. You mentioned Myers-Briggs. It has about 4,000 research studies and papers done on it, and with a massive amount of support behind it and proven results it's one of those fantastic tools that's used by about 2 million people every single year across the globe. So it's a very proven and a very powerful tool.

How it really works, and how it works especially for people who are looking for a fresh start, is it takes them as they are. There are a lot of psychological tests and clinical tests that give people negative results, such as you are extroverted or not, or you're not very good at this or you're not good at that.

Myers-Briggs, instead, focuses on what your preferences are as a person. So if money is not an object, if you weren't at work and you weren't influenced by anything from the outside world, what are your true preferences?

That's really closely related to the authentic self that I was talking about because it really gets down to the nitty-gritty of what your true preference is. That maps out a picture that is so clear that some people are really surprised about what their real preferences are in life and what their authentic self is, compared to what they're living.

They all of a sudden have something that tells them quite visually that they might not be living in their true authentic self. And that might be confronting for some, but for others, it's really empowering and freeing. They start to feel freedom for the first time. And then they start their journey towards being their authentic self.

And then, yes, you did mention some holistic, more creative, and more of the touchy-feely stuff. I have done this with some really hard corporate types. It's always really good fun because people approach these sort of creative, soft tools with a lot of skepticism. But these are probably the most powerful ones to change you because they start to get you dreaming again.

You mentioned earlier that people give up their dreams, especially when they become adults and they get forced into roles in their lives. They accept that as their reality and, all of a sudden, they let go of their childhood dreams.

Some of the tools that I teach and take people through are absolutely powerful in digging out some of those amazing dreams and giving shape to them. Understanding what's behind them and seeing how you can take a step towards them and that it's actually possible.

A lot of people think, "That's childhood stuff. That no longer relates to me. Or I don't know how to do that."

When people lock into that through these tools that I offer, it's very powerful and very exciting and people want to start a whole new job, career, path, or relationship. They go into a level that they thought that they would never be at.

So it's very powerful stuff.

So you're able to take this data and help people interpret, without judgment or any kind of prejudice as to what they should or shouldn't be doing. You just deal with the facts and reality of where they are and develop a plan for a Fresh Start from that point.

Is this a common point of the realization "if this hadn't happened to me, if this divorce hadn't happened, if this job loss hadn't happened, I may never have discovered this"?

Rachel Bandara: Absolutely. They might actually find themselves feeling quite relieved that they went through that, which sounds unbelievable, because divorces and job losses are quite traumatic things to go through for people.

But what I find is that people actually are quite relieved at the end. They say, "Oh, my goodness. If it weren't for this, I would have never found myself. If it weren't for this, I would have never come across this other opportunity." So, yes, it's absolutely right.

Do you feel that this might be the moment, and I know you talk about how great it is to be there and witness this, when those feelings of "change is impossible" or "I just don't see how I'm going to have the strength to work through this" start lifting as the Fresh Start becomes clearer ?

Rachel Bandara: Absolutely. One of the things that's really important to me if someone has completed the program and they've done the coaching sessions is when they go back out in to the world, they need to have that empowerment within themselves to be able to continue without me.

So if something happens to me, my clients will be able to keep going and keep growing in strength.

That's the whole idea of the program because a lot of traditional practices, and this is not a dig at traditional practices, but they are very coaching and counseling dependent. Which means you're dependent on the client coming back to you, time after time, month after month, sometimes for years. You as a client have to go back and keep going to weekly sessions or long term.

And that, to me, is not a very empowering state to be.

What is empowering to me is that the client is able to come and do a program. Get out there and now be empowered to walk the walk by themselves.

So that part is really important to me. And, yes, a lot of clients do find that they have everything they need now, especially because they started at that very basic level of taking them as they are, without any judgment. That is quite a relief to people to start at that and to not be judged for that.

They have the tools. They have the program. They can go out there and be empowered to do what they need to do without being dependent on counseling and weekly sessions.

Discovering this authentic self is exciting and it really does bring a very potent meaning to a Fresh Start.

You have people that think, "You know what? I'm ready. I want to make a fresh start. I see a target now. I see potential. I see opportunity where I didn't see it before."

Then they can fall into what you call the "cycle of perfection," that can throw a big wrench into so many well laid out plans. They jump into doing something new, but then it's got to be perfect.

How can the myth of perfection affect the progress of someone on this journey?

Rachel Bandara: At one point, I was the biggest perfectionist in the world, so this is very familiar ground for me. Having been stuck in that perfection cycle is absolutely horrific because you can stay there for years.

You think you're doing the right thing because, believe it or not, society actually thinks it's a good thing to be a perfectionist. There are certain rewards attached, especially in the work place, if you're a perfectionist.

So there's a certain amount of importance that's attached to it, and a certain amount of confidence and identity attached to that. This explains why it's so hard for people to get out of the cycle, because if they're conditioned to think that this is something that is really good, being a perfectionist, I've got to get this right. I've got to do this perfect. If it's not perfect, then it's not worth doing it.

Thinking like that lead people to be stuck in that cycle, consistently doing stuff, being busy but actually not getting the results that they need.

A good example is writing a book. For some people, it is a lifelong thing. They start to write the book and they will constantly nip away at it for years without actually getting it published. Now the reason for that is perfectionism.

What is amazing about the authentic self and the authentic identity work that I do is that people all of a sudden find that it's okay to not be perfect. This is a big revelation to a lot of people because society thinks being perfect is a good thing.

We're not meant to be perfect. We have our flaws. We have our differences. We have our different, unique colors and ways of doing things, and that's what makes us who we are.

Because the work I do is without judgment, people all of sudden feel that it's actually okay to be themselves. It is okay to get my book published as it is. It's actually okay for me to get up and sing and do a recording and do an album. Do whatever they've been dreaming of without just putting it off for another few years.

So, yeah, it's amazing to see people stepping away from that perfection cycle.

Obviously in the world of self-help, in the world of people that are in situations like this, easy answers are easy to find.

You're very clear that perfection is not going to be obtained and it does take real commitment, effort, and an investment of time and money. It's not as easy as "you read this passage, drink this potion and everything's going to change".

There are those that want and need something to change so badly, but just won't take that leap to make that investment of time or money, to make this change and discover this about themselves. What is it that they're missing out on when they just accept things the way they are or they do their best to go back to where they were, thinking that that is the answer?

Rachel Bandara: What they're missing out on is actually massive because, number one, they are thinking, "I've tried so many different things. I have read this book. I drank that magic potion and it didn't work." And like I said, somehow these things do cause more damage than good because people think that if they do read that book and do those things then everything will be fine.

But working on yourself actually takes time. We spend a lot of time working on a lot of other things in life. We work on our job. We spend time with family and friends.

So we spend a lot of time and the world is screaming out for our time. A lot of what we fail to do these days, especially in a really busy world, is taking some time out for yourself to work on yourself. That is such a huge challenge for people.

The amazing thing, though, is when people do decide "I'm going to set aside just 15 minutes for this and then I'm going to go on the program for this weekend or for these couple of days," and when they do make that time, it's far different from a self-help path. Because you're not really self-helping. You're not actually being told to read a book and all of your problems go away.

It's about finding out where you are and building on from that. I think a lot of clients, all of a sudden, see the reality, "I am important and my time is important. And if I don't look after myself, then I can't be the best of me and I can't give the best to my family and to my job."

There's actually a bible verse for that, as well which I'll paraphrase – You could gain the whole world, but you could lose your own soul.

That's where a lot of clients feel like they are at the moment. They're giving a lot to the outside world, but they're not giving enough to themselves. So when they set aside that time for themselves, then change can start to happen.

So many people find themselves in these situations that they feel are insurmountable and the opportunity to find someone like you that can help them through that is just tremendous.

What it is that led you to create a business around helping people through these situations? What is it that let you take what you learned from your own journey, that you applied to yourself and to take that and develop it into something that anyone can apply when they're in these situations?

Rachel Bandara: It starts with my own journey. I think it does for a lot of people who are out there doing stuff to help others. It is my own journey that defined how I get from where I am to where I want to be. Because I definitely relate to what my clients go through because I'm someone who had put away my creative side to be able to have a commercial, well-paying job and live a lifestyle that other people would look at and go, wow. That's amazing.

But when you're not being fulfilled and not feeling like I'm doing exactly what I'm supposed to be doing, that's a feeling that has been nagging away at me for a very long time.

Amazingly, this is such a common feeling. People just become blinded to it or they choose to push that away so that they can get on with their lives. That's what we choose to do.

I've done that. Even though, like I said, my commercial job has taught me some amazing skills, lessons and things that I actually use in my coaching for people to get results, what was really important for me was to tap back into that authentic self, which I had put away on the back burner. And to bring that out and be really honest with myself and see where I want to be in life.

From a young age I've worked with other young girls, in mentoring programs. When I was older and working in the commercial world, I ran mentoring groups for young ladies, and emerging leaders, and that sort of thing.

Throughout all of this, I could look back and see, yes, in all of these situations, I'm literally in mentoring and coaching situations no matter where I was or what my circumstances were.

That's when I finally realized it's what I'm meant to be doing because it gives me such a sense of reward and a sense of fulfillment. And to know that and to have reached that feeling is an absolutely amazing experience for me.

I think feeling that for myself on a daily basis made me want to start a business and to help others be able to get to that position themselves, to get on that journey themselves. Because it's actually not about getting to a position. It's about this whole journey that we're on. Once you're true to your authentic self, the opportunities that open up are truly amazing.

It's because I've experienced that for myself that I wanted to find a way to take people through the same process that I have refined for the last eight years or so.

Your results speak for themselves, such as some of the staggering transformations and discoveries people have made about themselves, and even going in a direction they probably never even conceived of, when this fresh start was thrust upon them.

How can people find out more about Rachel Bandara, what you're doing, and how they can get involved?

Rachel Bandara: It's an absolute pleasure to talk about something I really love and I'm passionate about.

For anyone who's interested in finding out a bit more, they can go to my website, http://www.RachelBandara.com. You will be able to sign up for a certain program, if you are interested in doing the program. If you're interested in one-on-one coaching, then you have the option to do that, as well. So that website again is http://www.RachelBandara.com.

About Rachel Bandara

Rachel is Sri Lankan born and New Zealand raised, Personal and Professional Development Coach, who specializes in Authenticity, Creativity and producing results for clients who are looking for a Fresh Start in life. She is a qualified MBTI (Myers-Briggs Type Indicator) Practitioner and an Executive Master Coach and has over a decade of experience in various industries such as Engineering, Finance, IT and Education as a qualified Project Manager.

DILANI first launched as a boutique image consulting company, through which she has conducted over 300 individual, corporate and group sessions in areas of Image, Confidence, Communication, Creativity, Authenticity, and Leadership. Her passion in developing people both in their personal and professional life, saw her developing programmes in the last few years through DILANI & Co. that empower people to achieve a deeper level of change and transformation in their lives.

Her expertise has seen her feature in international blogs, and as a keynote speaker and consultant, and in many mentoring programmes for women and young leaders. If you would like to book Rachel for an individual coaching session or plan, Group/Corporate sessions, Keynote Speaking, or like to inquire about her suite of Transformation products and programmes, please email info@rachelbandara.com.

WEBSITE:	RachelBandara.com
EMAIL:	info@RachelBandara.com
LOCATION:	Auckland, New Zealand
FACEBOOK:	Facebook.com/RachelDilaniBandara
TWITTER:	Twitter.com/RachelBandara

Stop Negotiating and Threaten Mediocrity

According to Renee Gambino, mediocrity is staying within the status quo and allowing it to make decisions for you. Business owners are faced with a dilemma when they stay in that mediocre place because it's safe and comfortable but contrary to their desire to grow and have the income and lifestyle that would truly impact their life and the lives of others.

Gambino believes that in order to succeed in a crowded marketplace, those who want to be successful need to stand out and step away from mediocrity. Individuals should connect with their born uniqueness to allow potential clients to notice them because that's when businesses grow and lives are lived full on.

It can be hard to step into the uncomfortable and Renee excels at helping business owners navigate these rocky waters and attain more success than they've ever had.

Conversation with Renee "The Bare Boss" Gambino

What is it about mediocrity that creates an obstacle and slows down so many hard-working entrepreneurs from reaching that success they set out to achieve?

Renee Gambino: My definition of mediocrity is staying within the status quo and allowing it to make decisions for you. Status quo comes from the Latin "state in which". 95% of the population makes less than six figures. 6% of the population makes a great living doing what they love. Those percentages together always blow my mind! That's what the statistics say is the "status quo". What the statistics don't measure is the innate massive potential we all have to be in full on control of our income and our outcomes. So, in order to threaten mediocrity, we have to challenge the status quo and start making decisions based on desired results. But, what happens is we tend to stay in that mediocre place because it's safe. Otherwise, we truly have to step up, stand out and get what we really want.

We have to step up and say, "Hey, I'm great at what I do, and I should get paid what I'm worth. *And* I'm okay with owning that."

That's the trouble spot for people where they really, really get stuck – making that decision and being a stand for, , "I'm going to stand out." I'm going to create offers and proposals that are high value AND position me as an expert. I see it all over the place, even in images in websites. People choose to create websites that look like other people's websites in their industry because that's the status quo. Safe!

So you end up in the mix with everybody else and that's where you'll always stay – in that state of not standing out. That's a problem.

It seems contrarian to when people think, "I'm going to go into business for myself, because I'm good at what I do and I can help people in a way others may not be able to help. I know I need to stand out so people will choose me."

Yet, the first decisions they make are based on "How can I blend in?"

Do you find that to be impeding their progress or success, rather than helping them launch their success?

Renee Gambino: Yes. It comes down to everything. What their business card looks like. What their clothing looks like. Just think about even going to a conference or a networking event or just walking around town as you're representing yourself.

If you're average, you're average. You see people, especially here in New York City, that allow themselves to stand out.

How someone can actually stand out in the middle of Times Square in Manhattan is pretty extraordinary. I always give that person an incredible amount of credit, because that's one of the most difficult places in the world to be "seen" and "heard."

Some people think that you need to be off the wall, or need to have been born "special," but that's not true. I never recommend people be really off the wall because then you come off as strange and weird. You don't want to do that.

But certainly, if everybody could connect with their actual uniqueness, that's exactly what would make a difference. That's when potential clients notice and want to say yes to working with you.

You describe how people work so much harder to blend in and don't get results, versus being their natural selves, which requires far less work. When they let that happen – some remarkable things occur.

It sounds simple to say 'be yourself,' but it's not simple for people to break out of the pack.

Renee Gambino: No. It's not at all because we generally see ourselves as "others have defined us."

When we take the steps to tap into who we were born to be, instead of who we think will be accepted, liked and loved, it's uncomfortable and unfamiliar, so we revert to comfortable and familiar. That's usually what we choose because we know our feet are on the ground when it's familiar. We feel unsteady when we step out of that.

But, that's the moment when growth actually happens. The more uncomfortable and unsteady we feel when we step into that, the more you know you're on the right track.

People just have to make that decision and say, "I know who I really am." It takes a some work. We don't just all of a sudden go, okay, I know exactly who I am and I'm ready to explode it!

But we can tell when we're struggling because it's going to happen in the results that we're getting. So there are areas, if you're not working with the clients that you want to work with, if you're not connecting and joint venturing with the kind of people that you'd like to, that means you're actually not being authentic because you really want those type of clients. You wouldn't want to connect with those types of people if it wasn't who you are. We tend to question if those are our "people" just because we get self-conscious and hold back waiting for something to be different or a "better time". We throw circumstances into the mix.

How did you recognize that you were working to try to hide from your true self?

Renee Gambino: Early on in my entrepreneurship (20 years ago), I found myself trying to find the right words and trying to make sure to impress. I literally felt like I just didn't belong in a highly intellectual conversation because it was too sophisticated and I wasn't that sophisticated. So, therefore, I didn't belong there.

It took me some time to recognize how much I had to offer. What people will find is that if they're in a group of different types of people, you're actually going to become more interesting by not being like them. You're even more accepted into that scenario when you're not engaging and using body language that says, "I'm so uncomfortable with myself right now that I wish I could disappear!"

I've had the opportunity and privilege of seeing you in live event scenarios and you definitely stand out.

One of the things that occurred to me when you talk about people, blending in and trying to fit that stereotype, is that the result is they become a "me too" business. There is very little that separates them from their competition.

Renee Gambino: Competition can feel fierce. But the real deal around it is no one can compete with you when you're super authentic and you have solid strategy and action in place. Nobody does you better! Competition can make business owners do strange things like negotiate their fees and time while doing everything possible to fit in.

When you put yourself in that "me too" situation, you can only separate yourself by price. How do you recognize and avoid the negotiable mindset that is the success killer for so many businesses?

Renee Gambino: Negotiable Mindset is my signature theory that I believe creates suffering for most people in general., Negotiable Mindset is being in agreement with accepting circumstances that keep you in mediocrity as truth. In business, those circumstances can look like "I can't charge that much, or power is pretentious. I don't want anybody to think that about me. Or I don't want to stand out too much because what will people think?."

It'll show up by negotiating your fees or starting to offer discounts. Or by creating things because other people are doing them and using other people's models. Now, I'm not saying reinvent the wheel in your industry, you do want to use strategy around that.

It starts to show up basically in how much money you're making and who you're working with. You continually work hard to fit in and stay in that status quo place. But what you're actually doing is making it more difficult for your potential clients to make a decision to choose to work with you.

It's very hard to make a decision if you're looking at five different mediocre businesses. Potential clients don't know how to assess the risk anymore of "Will they really do what they say they're going to do? Will I really get a return on my investment? I don't know who to choose."

So when people stop negotiating who they are, what they charge and what kind of value that they provide, people are able to make a decision. It actually makes it easier for potential clients. There's less stress over "I don't know if I should charge that much. Or I don't know if I should do this. Or I don't know if I should do that."

In reality, it's actually helping people to make a decision. We just get caught up on how we personally feel and what kind of value systems we have around the money mindset. We get in our heads and start forgetting about the potential client.

You have to help them make this decision. They're looking for someone help! Stop negotiating and start putting it out there so that they can say yes!

You just distilled down exactly what the value is that you create and the value that you provide to your clients is to be able to distinguish between being the best at what you do. People can work really hard to improve the tactical side of a business to get better at a skill, which often does absolutely nothing to increase the value or the business. It just makes it better in their mind and that's what so many people think they need to invest their time and money in.

But, like you said, it's about giving people a reason to choose you.

Renee Gambino: Yes. They're confused so they either choose nobody or they eventually find someone that's not negotiating their own value and providing delivery on their service. Just because you stand out doesn't mean people are going to stick with you. You must deliver on what you say. It ends the confusion for people, and that's what's most important because people are running around confused all day long.

So if you really want to help people, you've got to help them not be so confused. It's really interesting. That's when people get a sigh of relief and think "This person knows their stuff. This person knows exactly who they are. This person knows what they charge. I feel really good about that." People actually trust that more!

Like you said people get caught up in "I'll just get another certification or another degree or I'll take another class and I'll put another piece of paper on my wall."

We might say, "Oh, that person's the best at this, but that's because we had a personal experience with them." If you're walking around saying you're the best, no one's going to believe you anyway. It sounds like a gimmick.

So we can take that pressure off of us by knowing that people are not looking for the best. They're looking for a lot of value with someone they can trust to deliver. That's what it's all about!

Part of standing out is not only letting people see who you really are, but also being able to accept the fact that not everyone is going to like who you are. How do you deal with and accept that, and how do you help your clients accept that not everyone will like them?

Renee Gambino: If you're trying to fit in from every angle, you're going to make yourself crazy. Once again, that's where people get into that conflict of confusing other people and making their marketing near impossible to get a consistent handle on growing their income.

Part of the Negotiable Mindset is thinking that either we have to serve everybody or they're not enough people. Because most of the time, we're trying to be so generic that we're trying to serve every last niche we can get our hands on.

If you think about it, choose not to get really clear and stand up and be who you really are, you're going to attract potential clients that you don't even like or you don't want to work with. You want to work with people that get you, even if you're very different.

I'm very different to a lot of my clients. I'm more bold. I'm more on the edge. I'm not afraid to tell the truth and that's not the norm. I speak in bullet points. I ask powerful questions. I can tear something apart really fast and furious and get right down to the source of the problem. I'm about helping people as fast as possible. We don't want to drag this out.

But, I found in many areas of my life that people felt extremely intimidated by someone that was going around telling the truth. I got myself in trouble a few times.

What would actually happen is people would look at me and say, "I can't believe you just said that." And honestly, I would be like "Oh, I'm sorry. I thought I was just stating the obvious."

To me, it was like, "Isn't it just obvious that that's really what the problem is?" I wouldn't want to sugarcoat this or tap dance around it for a few decades like so many people do. Let's just get through this and move forward.

So it can happen that people, they just don't connect with you. But I'll tell you what, if there is someone that I have to tiptoe around or I have to change who I am and try and figure out how I'm supposed to phrase something or address something with them - I don't want to work with them.

We've all had clients that we were like, "Oh, my God. How did I find this person?" We say, "Never again. That personality type or that kind of person doesn't fit with me."

But what we did, in order to get that client, somehow, some way, we negotiated who we are and said, "Well, I don't want to lose the money. I don't want to lose the client. So I can deal with this."

Then we find out that it really doesn't work for anybody. So you do need to be careful with not stepping out and not being yourself, because of who you're going to attract. It can also hurt your reputation.

Honestly, in the end, when you're who you are and you stand in that, people know what to expect. They can refer to you because they know for a fact that the next person's going to get the same person. That's, again, how get known and businesses grow.

When you say helping people to decide, to give them a reason to make a decision about you – that may mean giving them a reason to decide not to work with you because you're not the type of person that they want to work with?

Renee Gambino: Absolutely. Everybody's so confused. Let's help the world by helping people be less confused. That's why so many people can't make a decision. I'm really comfortable with somebody saying, "You know what? You're not my style or you're not what I'm looking for," I'm like, "Oh, thank God we figured that out, because that's a good thing." I extend the same courtesy. If I don't feel someone is a good fit, I say no. I won't work with someone who's looking to skip doing the work but still get amazing results.

Did you ever think you might not be the best option for a client but then decide, "No, I'll be different for this person so I can make it work"?

Renee Gambino: Yes. I did that once a while ago. I honestly ended up with the client from hell and I knew it. We know when they're not our people.

But, what happens is we get really nervous about "I want to make sure that I grow my business. I don't want to say no. And I don't want people to think that I can't work with certain people." And I say, "Why not? Why not be clear?" It makes marketing so much easier, and it makes making money so much easier.

I might be really to the point and speak in bullet points. I love bullet points. When someone tells me some long story, I can give you two sentences and we just tore that sucker right down to the bottom.

It doesn't mean that everybody else is like that. It just means they appreciate that from me. I'm going to help them fast and furious and they can trust me that they're going to get the truth. That's why people like working with me. They don't need to be like me.

That's where business owners once again confuse themselves. They think that they need to be like their client. No, no, no. You just need someone that appreciates your style. People appreciate other people's styles. More than anything, they appreciate a unique style.

It's just the way other people are. We think we're supposed to be looking for ourselves. It's not true. You need to look for people who can appreciate who you are.

So many people are guilty of trying to appeal to the widest audience. They're trying to cast the widest net, which is oftentimes a fast path to that negotiable mindset.

Howard Stern is a great example. He's out there and probably 90% of the population can't stand him. But that's okay. He's extremely wealthy because of that. He has positioned himself for that 10% of the population that just absolutely loves and resonates with him. He's given them a reason to choose him.

Can you give another example of a celebrity that changed completely from what they thought they were supposed to be, to who they really are, and what the results of that have been?

Renee Gambino: My favorite example for that is Miley Cyrus. I find her so incredibly interesting. Also what's interesting about my interest in Miley is I'm not really a fan of her music and her style, per se. But I'm a fan of who she is. She started out this young girl with some talent and she started to put herself out there.

Then she started growing into her true personality. She got a little older, which gives people permission to put themselves out there. She really went the distance and she made a decision. But she did not care what anybody else thought. When she did that, people got really opinionated around this young lady. A lot of questioning and judging,

Miley did that one music video where she's literally naked, swinging on a wrecking ball and it was so controversial! Miley is a beautiful young woman and the girl's got talent. But, what it was is people couldn't believe how confident she was, and that was the problem. Not right or wrong, morally, ethically, any of that. The conflict was in her confidence.

Now what happened for her is number one, she got a ton of media coverage, right? We all know that when things get like that, the media loves it which is a beautiful thing for a young star.

Her ticket sales skyrocketed. Her fan base increased. And with it, she could not care about who doesn't like her music, or who doesn't like her style, or who doesn't like who she's become in the world. But you know what? Her arenas are full. Her album sales are sky high. She gets asked to host monstrous events, like the Grammys.

It's all because people can trust that Miley's going to be Miley. They can trust what she's going to deliver. They love her music. They love her. As far as Miley Cyrus is concerned, who cares what anybody else thinks because you can't fit the whole world in an arena anyway. There are only so many tickets to be sold.

Who she loves to be around is who she attracts, and that's what's so incredibly interesting about her. She became a super star when she became truly who she was.

She's young. She's got permission to over time change again. Who knows?

That's an excellent example, because she has all those elements that you've talked about. She has probably achieved a bigger success now even though she may have more people that actively dislike her.

Before, she had a mass of people that were probably just indifferent about her because she was another kid on a Disney show.

She didn't invest her time and money in becoming a better singer, right? Instead, she decided to be who she truly felt she was.

Renee Gambino: She's the best at being Miley Cyrus. That's who she's truly the best at being. And that's what we all need to decide and stop negotiating. We are the best at who we are and it is the only time and space in our lifetime that we will ever be the best.

You can be the best in your industry or the best in whatever service you offer. That's a perception anyway because that's not even real. The only real thing is us and who we are.

I think that what you've talked about can probably come down to taking responsibility and having accountability, rather than someone feeling they have to be whom the world, or the industry, dictates. Or, as you say, "The boss of you. The boss of your income. The boss of your outcomes."

You have three key components you talk about for people to use to eliminate the negotiable mindset. These are respect, connect, and affect.

When someone decides to become that boss, what impact does respect, connect and affect have on that decision?

Renee Gambino: They are really important, because they are the keys to eliminating Negotiable Mindset.

Each of those areas is twofold. It's tapping into yourself first and then how it applies to your clients/audience/relationships. It will make or break you when it comes to your desired results. It shows up in your marketing, messaging, money mindset, offers, proposals, relationships and your bank account.

It's always going to be a combination of mindset and skillset. When we look at respect, connect and affect, let's talk about the first thing, respect. We start with self-respect. That's number one. We have to decide we truly want.

Generally speaking, as business owners, when we decide what we want, we look at the business instead of what kind of lifestyle we want. We build our life around our business. It needs to be the other way around, or else you're not being self-respecting.

So you have to respect that you deserve and desire certain things and that's where you need to work FROM! Because a lot of times, people grow successful businesses, and they just can't wait till it's over so they can finally have a life.

When we're looking at respecting the client, because we respect ourselves, we respect our clients. So we deliver on what we promise. We offer what we're truly an expert at. Whether it's a handshake or a contract, you've got to deliver.

I decided that I'm going to be self-respecting by saying this is who I am, this is what I offer and this is what it costs, and in return, I respect my clients by delivering and doing what I say I'm going to do. It doesn't matter how big or small the promise is, you make sure it happens. You have to put strong processes and strong self respecting values in place for that. That's the first thing. It may be organizational processes, proposals, offers or sales process.

Next is connect. Connecting with self and your prospective clients. You'll start with what you really want meaning the money, lifestyle and clients, but that's when it hits you! You get in the middle of it and all of a sudden you're reverting back to your old ways of negotiating what you really want. So you have to connect! With yourself! You might even say, well why don't we do this first? It's because most people think they're all good with having lots of money, perfect clients and a life they love until they get into the thick of it! This is where I help people dig into what's holding them back so they can take the absolutely necessary steps to break free from mediocrity and be a stand for what they want! It's about being the Boss of your income and your outcomes! This is where I step in and do my magic!

This is what makes the difference! Believe me, if it were easy to do on your own, everyone would be there already!

It's about being honest with yourself. Me, I'm the boss. I'm authentic. Truth, bare, boss. You can always expect that from me because I tapped in.

I'm really authentic and you're always going to get my truth, like it or not. That's about tapping into who you were born to be. That's that unique, authentic place.

And with connecting with self, then you're able to connect with clients. So be real. You've got to connect on an emotional level and that means no tricks, no gimmicks, no negotiating. You've got to build trust. That's how you connect with people. By being trustful.

And that's so much easier when you're yourself.

Renee Gambino: You can't believe the pressure that it relieves. So many people are so nervous about being who they are, but when you're who you are the words flow, the people flow. You can sleep at night. You're not trying to figure out some way to maneuver around something or get something to work.

Just do your thing. Of course, you have to use strategy, steps and action in place! You're messaging must make sense to people. You do need to get help with that if you're unable to really make it rock solid.

When you're able to connect with clients, that's when you can affect them. That's the third part of having the income and life you really want. When you're connected with self and others, you're able to make changes for people. That's the AFFECT! People start getting what they want. These people start getting a return on their investment with you. That's when they start referring. That's when you start growing. That's when people want you around.

Then people start to call you when you start to be able to affect others. In turn, you're going to affect your own life. You're going to affect your income, who you're being, what you're doing and what you have, because that's when you can truly be able to share, save, invest. You've got to have an affect on yourself and others to gain momentum and traction in business and life!

That's the important part, when you talk about mindset, and skill-set. People will invest in their skillset, in the tactical part of the business, getting another certification, and things like that.

It seems that when people really see dramatic, even explosive growth, in their business is when they invest in the mindset part. This is exactly when everything comes together with the respect, connect and affect. You have a very concrete definition and understanding of the mindset of where you're coming from and who you're being with your clients.

That's a remarkable thing and I can see where that can have such a big impact and quick impact when people get that.

Why do you think people feel they aren't ready to move forward, or feel they just need to do it all on their own?

Renee Gambino: People think, "As soon as I make money, I will be able to have money." But you don't know how to get to where you want to go. That's going to cost you some money. That's the hamster wheel, once again. "I want to struggle. I'm going to suffer because I don't know any different."

We were taught if you work hard, you deserve the reward. It's not supposed to be easy. Life is hard. We also think as grown ups who own businesses that we're supposed to have all the answers. You don't have all the answers and you're not supposed to..

This is a very serious problem for small business owners. You don't want to be seen as someone that can't handle something. You can't understand why you can't do it yourself, because you're a very intelligent person. You know how to do what you do, but there are other aspects of your business that you just don't get. You're smart and it's frustrating.

It's just that we were taught that it's very honorable to do something on our own. We're usually taught that by someone who doesn't have a very successful business.

It's our parents. It's our grandparents. It's our family, teachers, people we see out in the world. If you asked someone with a very successful business, they would tell you the truth. And the bottom line is, you must have other people around you. You must get the support you need so that you can be who you are and grow your business.

No successful business owner will ever say, "Oh, you need to do this on your own. Don't invest in yourself. Don't hire people. Don't do get help."

But it lives really deep within us and it's hard to let it go.

Right. It seems like those are stories that people tell themselves.

One of the things that I love is you dig deep into the layers of the real reason, not the reasons people tell themselves – "I need to do it on my own" or "I need to make more money first."

You've identified that at the core of this is that people may not really fully trust that they can achieve those goals that they set for themselves, based on maybe something that happened in their past or while growing up. That fear of the unknown is almost like a protective layer. People think "If I don't try, if I don't put myself out there, then I can't fail."

Renee Gambino: Right. You won't get hurt. So the only way that we can have any belief around what we're able to achieve is to actually have the experience. This is the glitch. We have to have the experience before we can believe that we can have the experience.

That's where it takes the support to help people through that process, so they can have the experience of growth, of closing clients that they never thought they could close before, offering offers they never thought they could offer before, or being who they truly are because they never had that experience.

Once you start breaking through that and stepping out into that uncomfortable place and starting to make things happen, that's when the confidence starts shooting through the roof. That's when people start playing bigger and bigger and bigger. Because they say, "I got this."

The only difference between the people that have big success and the people that struggle on a daily basis are they just decided to have one good experience, then another good experience, and another good experience faster and concentrated. That's the only difference.

It's really valuable that you are able to provide that path, because a lot of people never realize this is within their reach.

Renee Gambino: Once we raise awareness, that's when we can make a change. A change in the state in which we're currently in. In my businesses, it's the state of who you're being, your income and how it's impacting your life. You can't actually help anybody do anything. You must create high levels of awareness so they can figure out where they are actually are. Because when you say map, you're correct. When you have that high-level awareness, you know exactly where you are. Now, you can pinpoint that on the map. Now you can get to where you want to go.

If you don't actually know where you are, well, you're lost.

Unfortunately, that's where a lot of people find themselves.
So what led Renee Gambino to create this business that helps people with this? How did you come to recognize this in yourself and realize that you can help others with this as well?

Renee Gambino: Before I was doing this, I was in holistic health for nineteen years. I did a lot of body work. I owned a really successful wellness center and I had all kinds of practitioners working for me.

But one of the conflicts I had, and I didn't even actually know I had for quite a while, was I would feel guilt around the fact that I did not fit in to the average holistic health provider package. I wasn't really "woo woo." I was a very loud mouth, Italian girl that probably cursed more than she should have.

But, I was extremely goal oriented and extremely client-centered. I finally learned how to respect my time and respect my fees. I had these clients just coming, coming and coming. It was almost magical. I felt really guilty in the industry, in general, that I wasn't "like everybody else." Because you're supposed to be soft and loving, holistic, and it just wasn't me.

I didn't hang out with other holistic health providers. I didn't get them because I always saw them as, I hate to say this, but broke and flaky, but definitely going to heaven.

What I realized, what made me so successful, was I was not the stereotype and I refused to stereotype myself because it just wasn't me. I actually ended up in the end recognizing that my clientele was 90% entrepreneurs or CEOs. When I a realized that, I thought, "Wow. Like attracts like."

They just appreciated who I was and that I delivered when they came in. I could figure out the source of the problem fast, no matter how complicated. I deeply understood the process of breaking it down to simplicity, find the source of the problem and create an environment for healing. I was creative with what I did. I was always there. I was on time. I had all these standards in the environment and that's what they loved.

I recognized that after 19 years of that, it wasn't what I wanted to do any more. I decided that I would step back and see what made me so successful at this. When I started really peeling it back, I recognized that I had this innate ability to connect with people and help them through whatever process they needed to. And in that case, it was bodies.

What I recognized was the body has the innate ability to heal itself, if given the right environment. So does a business. So does a relationship. So does a bank account – if given the right environment.

I just understood that I knew this on such a deep level and so I wanted to continue this because it works!

But I will tell you that when I first started doing this, I put myself in a box.

It was making my skin crawl to the point where I was like I think that maybe this isn't for me. Then I recognized from working with my mentor that the problem was that I wasn't being me and I wasn't putting myself out there in a truly authentic way. I was worried about what other people thought and wanted to fit in.

I had never done that before - tried to be somebody else. That's when I recognized who I am, is who I am. I was born a Gambino and that means something. When you're a Gambino, you live a certain lifestyle. You grow in a certain way, in a certain culture. It's who I was born.

I'm not bossy. I'm boss – and that's different. People appreciate that and trust and respect that with me. That's when I gave myself permission to be who I was. That's why I put myself out there now. Authentic, truth, bare, boss, take it or leave it.

Well, I can certainly say that the people that I've seen that have worked with you, the people whose businesses are transitioning, the clients you have, walk with a different swagger. They have a different confidence. That confidence isn't because they got better at what they did, but they got better at being who they are.

Renee Gambino: Thank you. Yes, it's exciting. There's nothing better than a client that contacts me and says, "I did it. I totally did it. I went in there. Did a presentation. I stood strong. I added value. I didn't negotiate. And I closed it for more than double what I would have normally charged."

Then all of a sudden, it's another case. It appears magical for people. I get so excited for them when they feel it. They have that experience. They feel really in control of who they are and they're happy to wake up and do it again.

That is a remarkable story to see this.

If people are ready to threaten mediocrity and start being who they really are, how can they find out more about Renee Gambino and get involved?

Renee Gambino: I'm easy to find. They can go right to http://www.ReneeGambino.com.

About Renee "The Bare Boss" Gambino

Renee grew up "Gambino" and learned from her beloved business-minded father, about never taking no for an answer and never caring what anyone thinks when it comes to having what you really want! In her words, "My Dad never won any awards for verbal finesse, but he taught me how to be a stand for myself, because nothing is worse than letting fear and weakness decide how you're going to live your life! My Dad in his way showed me how mediocrity will keep us small and lost in the mix. He told me I was a Gambino, and that means something. He died showing me the potential of the human spirit and how you never negotiate who you are or what you want! I miss that man!"

Renee had to overcome challenges living with a family name that showed up in the newspaper headlines being targeted for shakedowns, gambling and racketeering. Having a name deemed "mobsters" and "thugs" along with movies, t.v. and books that continued to remind her of how her family was seen in the world. Renee says "Even my Mom would remind me not to be like "Those Gambinos!" She suffered from over-controlling man, be quiet wife syndrome. Mom has since decided she has a voice and she knows how to use it!" Renee decided very early that she was as strong, savvy and badass as the men in her family! Renee explains it like this…"We lived by the family code, but my father didn't have any shovels in his trunk!"

Renee's secret weapon is her innate ability to see what others can't, and pinpoint blocks at record speeds. That's what ignites people to be more, do more and have more! She gets real with her clients and audience so they can prosper in the real world. Thoughts plus actions equals results. Renee brings the truth about how our minds work to engage sustainable change wrapped in proven, creative and rock solid strategies!

As a Powerhouse Speaker and Income Breakthrough Strategist, she's the Business Coach On Call for New York's number one talk radio WOR 710, I Heart Radio and Boost Radio, she's featured monthly in Change Your Attitude Change Your Life Magazine and has been interviewed for such shows as Leaders In The Trenches. She's currently working on her first book project that's planning on gaining traction to start an entire movement that threatens the trend of mediocrity!

As an entrepreneur for 19 years, Renee broke free of the paradigm, holistic business owner stands for "Broke, flaky, but definitely going to heaven!" For 11 years, her results driven, client-centered vision and business expertise built a multi-practitioner center leveraging a client base of 3000.

Since retiring from holistic health, Renee is now committed to having a part in creating a world that's free of limitations, and committed to spending her life living full on with her son Alec and her husband Alen Bonjolo, her number one fan and love of her life.

WEBSITE: ReneeGambino.com

EMAIL: TheBoss@ReneeGambino.com

LOCATION: Saugerties, NY

FACEBOOK: Facebook.com/TheBareBoss

LINKEDIN: LinkedIn.com/in/ReneeGambino

TWITTER: Twitter.com/ReneeGambino

Achieve Peak Performances

Mike Gillette is a master at helping others attain peak performance. He has become a master of everything he has ever done – black belts, counter-terrorism consultant, SWAT team commander, Guinness World Records – you name it, he's mastered it.

His incredible background has equipped him with the knowledge and experience to now help others achieve their most desired goals.

His mission is to affect positive change in others using the unique strategies he's developed. Through his intensive coaching approach, Mike draws a roadmap for clients to guide them towards their own personal successes.

Conversation with Mike Gillette

As a peak performance coach, you actually help people that are already good at what they do, but they see much bigger potential and just can't seem to figure out how to reach that potential. Can you describe type of clients you work with, and how you help them reach their peak potential?

Mike Gillette: Well, the first thing you mentioned is the term "peak performance." So let's get clear on what exactly that means. Peak performance is operating at your optimal level of potential and being able to get to that point in a consistent and systematic way.

For example, we all have had moments in our lives when what we're doing seems to go very well. Where what we want to have happen, happens. And it does so in almost effortless way. This is when we are in what psychologists refer to as a "flow state". Being in a flow state is an example of peak performance in action.

But, how does a person get to such a state? How does a person reliably re-enter that state? And how can they integrate that state into whatever it is that they do, whether they're an engineer, musician or competitive athlete?

I do this through a process which incorporates many of the methods that I've been introduced to which are somewhat unique to me. These various methods are not something I have invented. But, because I've been exposed to so many different things throughout my professional life, I've been able to extract what works well and combine them in a way that is understandable and attainable for regular people.

If a person is progressing along in their career, but they're trying to get to that "next level", one of the things I do is help them figure out what that next level is. What does it represent? Why do they want to get there? How will they know when they've gotten there? And so forth.

Once we flesh those things out, we devise a plan to get to that point. A lot of the things I've accomplished in my own life were the result of being good at planning and being good at execution. When people have a roadmap, we find that they do much better in terms of getting to the outcomes that they desire.

A lot of successful people find themselves humming along in that flow state, or flow zone. People know it exists, but don't know how to get into that zone.

In your experience as a paratrooper, SWAT commander, and counter-terrorism consultant, you've had to be able to put yourself in the zone almost at will, and it really is a mindset thing. Would that be how you would characterize it - being able to put yourself in that right state of mind when it's needed?

Mike Gillette: Mindset is everything. One of the challenges with working with someone, regardless of the area they're interested in working on, is the notion that they can control the direction of their mind. But they can. We all can. We can all take deliberate control of our thoughts if we choose to.

And once we begin doing this, we can start to exert influence over our emotions, such as our emotional responses to various circumstances. Ultimately, this allows us to get out of our own way and put a laser beam onto the target that we want and to work methodically towards it.

When people want to hire a coach, a lot of times, their mindset is "I need to hire someone to be accountable for my results, for my actions."

In shows like 'The Biggest Loser,' people are essentially surrendering their accountability to someone else to whip them into shape and to be there to ride them sixteen hours a day to make certain that they achieve whatever goals they set out to do.

Obviously, that's not sustainable. How do you define the role of a coach?

Mike Gillette: People get confused about what the role of a coach actually is. A lot of people are not actually looking for a coach, what they're really looking for is a boss.

A boss is different from a coach. A boss imposes external standards or expectations upon a client. The inherent problem here is that a client can be cajoled and harassed into compliance for a period of time. But these changes ultimately don't really belong to the client because they had to be beaten into the client in a manner of speaking. Therefore, the client doesn't own their outcome.

The difference between boss and a coach is that a coach facilitates. A coach provides a framework, a process. It must be up to the client to be accountable for their own dreams because nothing is more personal to you than your goals and dreams.

A coach is there to provide the roadmap to guide the process. And if the process isn't working, the coach adjusts course and continues to refine the route from here to there. Does that make sense?

It definitely does. In the business world, it would be like comparing an employee with an entrepreneur. Even successful CEOs still ultimately have someone telling them what to do, where to do it, what needs to be done, and providing that framework. The consequence of not working within that framework is unemployment.

Entrepreneurs are in a completely different place. They wake up every morning unemployed. It's up to them to be their own boss, set their own responsibilities, and set those benchmarks.

It seems what you are able to do with people is give them the tools and the power and the ability to be able to set their own benchmarks and to do the things that are necessary for them to get themselves to reach those benchmarks, without having someone else taking away their accountability.

Would that be the right way to characterize that?

Mike Gillette: I think that's a great way to characterize it. I look at it in terms of "What is it that you really want, even when no one is around to acknowledge it?"

Everyone knows what is expected of them, whether it's from friends, family members, their work place, or the norms of our culture. We all know what those things are. But, those aren't the things that really drive us on the inside.

The things that are personally important, those are the things that I'm well-suited to help people work towards. It's a combination of having some fairly novel approaches in which to pursue those things and that people look at me as someone who has overcome difficulties while accomplishing a variety of challenging things.

When I first started getting involved with coaching, it was really as an extension of what I did in law enforcement and as a tactical trainer. I was coaching, if you will, law enforcement officers and military personnel, taking people who were already very good at certain things and making them better.

One of the key pieces of my definition of peak performance is the integration of the mind with the body. This is not to suggest that everyone I work with is an athlete or becomes an athlete. Their own interests would dictate that. But, I deal with the body as well as the mind. I have exercises that unify the functionality of both, because I really look at them as one and the same. The body is the mind. The mind is the body. That is how I approach what I do. And I carry this same approach into what I do as a coach.

Here's an example of the boss dynamic in action, from a moment in time when I really noticed the disconnect that some people can have between their mind and their body. In 2007, I was working with a group of athletes on a reality-television show called Fight Girls. It was a competition-based show where all the competitors lived together in a house in Vegas. There were weekly eliminations so it followed a typical reality-show framework.

I was serving as a nutritionist for these athletes. These were all experienced kick boxers who were all gunning for an opportunity to go to Thailand and fight there, which is the homeland of international kickboxing.

These young women were smart. They knew about health and nutrition. But some of them would tell me something that I found absolutely perplexing. They would say, "Mike, tell me what to eat." So I would say, "You're an experienced athlete, you've studied this sort of thing. You already know what to eat."

Then they would say, "I know that I know what to eat. I want you to tell me." So they were aware what they were asking for. But, they were still asking. This circumstance gets back to the fact that some people actually want a boss rather than a coach. However, most people seem to respond better to a mentor or a coach. And that's the bandwidth that I occupy.

The results from the people that you work with speak volumes to your method. The accountability aspect is probably one of the most significant pieces. You stated that ultimately they're accountable to themselves. You are really there to guide them along their path, whatever that is.

Once they understand that they are responsible for their own outcome and they take that accountability, they're not looking to you. This is when the real work begins and that's where the real transformation begins.

What do you see as being the biggest obstacles to them actually reaching the real achievable potential that they have in them? What is it that you see stopping them, outside of the accountability?

Mike Gillette: Excellent question. Everybody has a dream, although we all know plenty of people who don't pursue their dreams.

So most people need to become comfortable with the idea of pursuing their dream in the first place. This usually comes after a coach has already asked questions like, "What do you want?" "How do you want things to be?" "What does this mean to you?" "Why does this matter?" and so forth.

After we've gone through those types of questions and we're really clear on what the client wants, then the coach can say, "You *can* have this. Not only can you have it, you *should* have it."

A coach can serve to grant that permission. Not that permission is ever actually required, but so many people feel as though they need it. We often look for external validation of what we want because we might think it's frivolous or selfish or something else.

This is what a coach can prospectively offer a client. The difference, at least with me, is after we establish that they can have it, that it's possible and it's worthwhile – then we get to the second piece.

The second piece is simply: Do you *really* want this? Are you willing to do whatever it takes? Will you go at this until you get it?

They have to answer those questions. They have to realize that it is up to them. It is the work that will get them there. Their work. It's not a magic wand. It's not a boss yelling them into compliance. It's them being accountable for what they want.

If they get that - if they get that the goal is important and that it belongs to them alone – that's when things can get amazing. But they have to be at that point. They have to be ready to not only hear that message, but they have to be ready to act on that message.

That is probably a big reason people get on this path to failure, for lack of a better word. That's what a lot of people are afraid of – failing. A fear of failure will keep them from even attempting something.

One of the things that you've identified, that is extremely telling, is that it seems that you believe that a half-hearted attempt could be more damaging than no attempt at all because it can begin that pattern of failure that they keep replaying. Is this correct?

Mike Gillette: That's absolutely correct. Many people will try things. And that's a word I don't really like because the word itself, "try", implies failure.

So people try things. But, even with productive intentions, if the plan they were pursuing wasn't a good one, then their attempt is likely to have ended in failure. And if they tried more than once and failed each time, they were ultimately reinforcing the notion that what they were pursuing was impossible. It's what leads people to say things like, "I can't have this. This is for other people, not for me."

Exactly. So many people have experienced this. They try to lose weight and they can't. So they simply say, "Well, I guess I'm just at my fighting weight, you know? This is what I'm supposed to be." Or, "Here I go again."

Mike Gillette: Right. We start rationalizing where we're stuck at.

You warn people – don't give it a half-hearted attempt because you're actually creating a damaging pattern there. But, a lot of people have already been down that road. They've done the half-hearted attempts. They started that pattern. They started replaying that tape.

A lot of people get to the point where they feel that this is just who I am. These are the cards that life has dealt me and this is what I have to live with. But you say, no. And you've proven that change is actually possible even after this repeated pattern.

Do you see that as being a misconception or something that people have just ingrained in their head, "This is just who I am and it's not something that can be changed?"

Mike Gillette: Very much. And it can be linked to a number of things, such as the unsuccessful previous attempts that reinforce a sense of inevitability. It can also come from people in your own social circle. I don't want to seem stuck on the topic of weight loss, but almost everybody brings it up as a topic and it has a visual element to it, making it easy to visualize.

So if you were to tell someone, "I'm thinking about going on a diet" - what will most people say? "Oh, you look fine the way you are." "Don't get too carried away." "You better be careful." Rather than encouragement or support, you're likely to hear all these cautionary comments.

All of these remarks are examples of the subtle attempts that people make to keep other people in their circle from doing things which result in change. Because if one person goes on a diet then they're going to make other people around them feel bad, the people who don't want to do anything.

As you can see, there are a lot of places where obstacles can come from. My job as a coach is to find those places. To break them down and confront people with a particular reality. Which, even though it's a positive reality, can still be a scary reality. The reality that, "Yes, you actually can have this." But this is, of course, only true if the person really wants it. Because if they don't really want it, they won't do what's necessary.

And there's also fear. I think that much of the clichéd phrase "fear of success", has to do with the fear of potential change. Change is scary to people because they don't know what it's going to be. They just know it's going to be different. And maybe they're not ready for different.

But to get someone to accept and embrace the unknown and totally immerse themselves in the solution to whatever their situation is can be scary. But that's what it takes.

I have been told that I'm an intense guy. The way that I approach my life and my goals reflects this. The things that I do are really metaphors for this kind of living. When you do the kinds of things that I do, you cannot hold anything back. There are no half-hearted attempts at breaking stacks of bricks with your body. There are no half-hearted attempts at bending steel bars. To be successful, you've got to be mentally committed, to be in the moment. It is by being in the moment and knowing that you've surrendered yourself completely to change, that change happens.

I think some people are afraid of throwing themselves at something so hard that there's no excuse. Because they still may not get it. But this is the bandwidth where high achievers live.

For example, there are many talented musicians out there, but not everybody is trying to win a college scholarship. There are a lot of scholarship musicians out there but not all of them are attempting to compete in international music competitions. The higher and higher you go, the greater the potential reward is. Conversely, going higher and higher can represent a greater sense of failure, if that is how you perceive such things.

But here is the key, if what you focus on is the pursuit of excellence, you can never fail. But if you pursue the arbitrary mileposts of what other people use as markers of success, you're always going to be unsatisfied.

We live in a society where Easy buttons, magic pills, and weight loss options are available at every turn.

Easy answers sell solutions. Easy answers sell products. They sell coaching. They sell services. They sell everything that obviously doesn't fulfill and often leaves people in a much worse spot than they began with.

But you don't mince words. You tell people that it takes effort and commitment to do this. So many people say, "Oh, I need to quit smoking. I'll go to the hypnotist and he'll zap me and I'll be all better," or "I need to lose weight. I just need to eat this prepackaged food and take this pill and boom. It's gone."

You offer none of that. You offer real answers, real solutions to problems.

Do you have people that come to you saying, "Just do what you do and make me successful. Make me happy."?

Mike Gillette: Absolutely. There's a certain visibility associated with some of the things I do. And people don't have an easy explanation for it. How does a guy who didn't even start pursuing feats of strength until he was 46 (I'm 53 now) do these things? There's no magic to it. I just do it.

That's what I bring to my clients. The mindset of "We're just going to do this. There is a goal and a plan and we're going to get you to where you want to go." That's a completely different mentality than magic pills and easy answers.

Helping someone transform into the type of person that does what needs to be done to make it happen is magic all in itself. It's also more powerful and long lasting than any type of magic pill or hypnotist session.

What is it that led you to do what you do? What led you to take your experiences with working through obstacles and beating the odds in so many things to helping others do the same thing and really transform and improve their lives?

Mike Gillette: I'm happy to share that. When I was a very young person, as a kid growing up, things were very difficult for me. I was scared. I felt helpless. We had all kinds of violence and chaos in our household. I internalized a lot of that negativity and that negativity manifested in some pretty predictable ways during my teen years.

When things were kind of at a critical point, I was eighteen years old and I attempted to kill myself. But, I somehow survived ingesting a bottle of painkillers chased with alcohol in a cheap hotel room by the interstate.

And after surviving that night, I reexamined my life and where I was going. I reconnected with a girl I had known, a girl who has now been my wife for over 30 years. We started going to church. She took me and it stuck. It changed my life. At that point, I decided that I wanted to help other people. I wanted to basically flip my life around from what it had been.

How did I pursue helping people early on? I joined the army. Then came college. After that was 12 years in law enforcement, then tactical training for a couple of years and bodyguard work for five years after that. Being of service has always been an underlying objective of mine.

I've always felt I was at my best when I was helping other people. And I've always felt I was at my best when I was pursuing strength. When I say that, I don't mean just in the physical context, but doing things that made me *better*. Better as a friend, as a neighbor, as a parent, as a husband. This has been an ongoing pursuit for me.

In the nineties, I started training law enforcement, corrections and military personnel. I found that I approached training in a very holistic way. I studied various disparate-seeming disciplines. I looked at behavioral psychology, hypnosis and neuro-linguistic programming. And I was likewise exposed to aspects of personal development through my martial arts training.

This is the way that my brain seems to work, I see how things connect. Regardless of the specific discipline, I was finding ways to connect what I was learning and using it to enhance what I taught to others.

Post-9/11, I started working with the private sector. I did a lot of work with the airline industry and the Disney Company as they sought to protect their operations from potential terrorist attacks. This was a shift of sorts for me as I was now working with civilians. And to do so I was still drawing from my "scary" and "dangerous" background but I was using that information to affect positive change, in an entirely different context.

This has been a constant, leading to the present day. I started teaching over 20 years ago. Working with people who were already operating at a high level and I was taking them even farther. And if I can help people like that, then imagine the margin for improvement with regular people who are new to such training concepts.

Even though a lot of the stops I've made along my way while building my resume may seem unconventional, I see them as being very much connected. They've all led very organically to the kind of work that I do now.

Without a doubt, there's absolutely nothing that can duplicate the experiences that you've had. It's a tremendous gift to be able to share that and let others benefit from that experience without having to be in the perilous situations that you've obviously put yourself in to achieve that.

How can folks find out more about Mike Gillette, what you're up to, your philosophies, and really about how to begin transforming in a way that you've put out there?

Mike Gillette: To find out more about what I do via coaching, along with links to other content, please visit my website at: www.MikeGillette.com.

About Mike Gillette

Mike Gillette has a life story that reads like an action-adventure novel. A life which has proven to be his own best case-study for goal attainment. He was a poor, scared and scrawny kid who grew up amidst a backdrop of extreme violence and substance abuse. A kid who would ultimately become an Army Paratrooper, SWAT Commander, Government Counter-Terrorism Consultant, Bodyguard to Fortune 500 CEOs, and a Record-Breaking Strongman whose feats have been documented by Guinness World Records and Ripley's Believe it or Not. As both practitioner and purveyor, Mike is a peak-performance pioneer. At over 50 years of age, he continues to transcend his own personal limits while teaching others how to do the same.

WEBSITE: MikeGillette.com

EMAIL: info@MikeGillette.com

LOCATION: Cedar Rapids, IA

FACEBOOK: Facebook.com/Mike.Gillette

LINKEDIN: LinkedIn.com/in/MikeGillette

TWITTER: Twitter.com/Gillette_Mike

YOUTUBE: Youtube.com/user/MikeGilletteTV

INSTAGRAM: Instagram.com/Mike.Gillette

Abolish Comfort Triggers and Maintain Weight Loss

Renée Jones is a weight loss counselor who is an expert at not only getting the weight off, but maintaining it over the long haul – something that is very rare and hard to do.

An ordained minister with a Masters in Marriage and Family Counseling and a Clinical Residency in Pastoral Care, Renée Jones engaged in the same battle faced by many, the inability to maintain weight loss.

Having figured out the triggers that lead to eating "comfort foods" that make someone feel better, she is now helping the masses conquer this problem by identifying these triggers. She then helps them retrain their mindset to find other ways to meet their emotional needs, rather than food.

Her unique approach to setting goals, in addition to her definition of rewards, makes this a win-win approach for all who seek to lose weight.

Conversation with Renée Jones

There is so much associated with the psychological piece of food and what we eat, how we eat, and how we think about food. You call it triggers for comfort eating.

How strong are these triggers and how do you help people recognize that this is the core of their problem?

Renée Jones: Mothers often give their children a pacifier. So, people get in the habit of when something is bothering them, they put something in their mouths for comfort. Our metabolism may be able to absorb the extra calories for a couple of decades.

Definitely, by forty, your metabolism doesn't help you out as much as it did, and your body doesn't necessarily use all the calories you're taking in. Yet, we still have the habit of putting something in our mouths for comfort. It could be a cigarette, it could be a drink, or it could be food of any kind. Very often, it's something that is sweet or salty. Even more often, it's something that we learned to depend on as a child.

So when you're feeling stressed, you put something in your mouth. When you're feeling lonely, you put something in your mouth. When we're feeling whatever, we tend to then put something that has an emotional attachment to it in our mouths. Over time, it shows up on our hips and thighs and everywhere else.

Talk about that attachment, because here's where the struggle is. You've gone through the struggles. You say your first diet started when you were ten years old and a lot of people can connect with that and recall their first diet. No one's ever gone on one diet, lost the weight and there it is – it's done.

Renée Jones: I'd love to meet the person for whom that worked. I was on a diet perpetually from the time I was ten until I turned fifty. I actually met my goal weight a week before my 50th birthday.

So it was always a struggle. It was a family struggle. I'd be standing there in the pantry or in front of the refrigerator just staring longingly, looking for something, and food's just easy. What we're looking for isn't actually in the refrigerator or pantry, but it's the easy substitute to get that need met.

Telling this is so powerful to a lot of people because it's something that a lot of people struggle with silently.

A quote I remember that I'll paraphrase is, "It's easy to lose weight. I've done it many times."

People get to the point where they say they're going to tighten up their belts, roll up their sleeves and do it. Then it becomes a chore when they have to maintain it.

It seems that something occurs that makes them go back to those triggers for that comfort food. What is it that causes people to bounce back? What do you see that can help people recognize when that's occurring?

Renée Jones: I suffered through that myself, particularly when I got to my goal weight because that was the thing I was looking toward.

The idea of a goal is that there's a finish line and when you reach the finish line, it's done. So you go back to whatever you were doing before, which is what got us into the place that made us so uncomfortable.

We need to start thinking about when you get there, make good choices to help you stay there. For example, think about moving across the country. You don't keep going back to L.A. if you live in New York.

One of the things that people often think is, "I'm being deprived. Everybody else gets a banana split. Why don't I get one?" Instead, you need to say, "No, this is how I eat. I'm not deprived." You certainly can have one special treat, but have only one and don't have it every day.

I think the thing is we just go back to the food habits that were making us miserable before because we've not had those "treats" for so long. Unfortunately, with triggers and with trigger foods, we are trying to get our needs met through food. We can limit that for a while, but until we deal with what's behind that and what's driving that behavior, then it's very hard to maintain.

When someone reaches their weight loss goal, how can they reward themselves without falling back into those old bad habits?

Renée Jones: There is a famous quote that says the reward is the act of having done it. My body is now my reward. The fact that I can now go buy clothes in a smaller size and the fact that I feel really good are my reward. I feel lean, I feel healthy, and I feel like I look good in my clothes. That is the reward rather than chocolate cake or an extra glass of wine.

You need to find rewards that actually support your new habits. The way we eat has to become a habit, rather than, oh, I'm just doing this for a short while.

To a lot of people, food is almost like a drug. It seems like there's a point in every meal where it stops being fuel for the body and becomes pure entertainment.

A lot of people associate that food with a romanticized vision. A pizza doesn't equal a pizza. A pizza equals a memory of some great time, or it represents something good that made something bad go away.

You help people choose to back out of the refrigerator or the pantry when they're staring and they're looking for that comfort. They're not really looking for food, but they're looking for the feeling or the memory or whatever romanticized vision they have that is associated with that food.

How do you get them to either lose or diminish that equation of food with that romanticized vision and make a better choice?

Renée Jones: That is crucial. I have an emotional attachment to peanut butter. I love it. It is wonderful. And it's nutritious in certain amounts. But what I finally figured out was it's a connection to both my mother and my grandmother, both of whom have now passed away. My mother passed away before my grandmother.

So any time I feel lonely or without them or I just want to talk to them, I would somehow find myself walking to the refrigerator to get to the peanut butter. I thought, "Wait a minute. You've got to take that feeling out of that jar and put it back in your heart where it belongs. Peanut butter doesn't bring them any closer to me."

The peanut butter was just sort of a comfort thing, but I can find better ways to meet that need than stuffing my face. One of my taglines is "Face your stuff. Don't stuff your face." It's so easy to stuff our faces, rather than sitting down, thinking about it, or talking with somebody about what it is that particular food is actually doing for you.

It made me fat. It helped me regain pounds somewhere along the way and back again. It's not the actual food, it's just what that represents for me. That was one of those times when I had to spend a long time working out what does it mean to me, and how can I get this need met in another more helpful way? How can I choose a better fix for that?

You've helped people with other addictions – for example, smoking or drinking. The one thing that separates food from a smoking or drinking addiction is that we don't need cigarettes and alcohol to sustain life. We can completely eliminate them, as hard as it may be. But with food, it's almost like an addiction that you have to manage because you can't eliminate it entirely.

How do you get past that, and how do you help your clients manage this?

Renée Jones: Different people have different ways of doing that. I think that's one of the keys. You have to figure out what actually works for you. Some people can say, "I'm never buying the trigger foods again." Some people will say, "Well, that's a part of who I am, so I have to find a way to manage it."

For me, I stopped buying peanut butter for a good six months to put a break in there. So, sometimes it is eliminating temptations from your environment, whether that's at work or at home or wherever. Just make sure you don't have those things around you. Because once they're not there, you either shift that to another food that then becomes a problem, or you have to figure out what you need that you're trying to find within that food.

That's one of the things that I help my clients figure out, okay - what works for them? How can we get this need met so that it does exactly what you want for you? Or you find a way to manage your consumption. And we'll work with that, too.

And you said something that's very important when you said that people are different. Everyone's different. And a lot of people, when they think about weight loss, they may think, "Oh, here's another diet or here's another program."

People usually want to buy a program – a very regimented or detailed diet so they don't have to think about what they're doing. They want to be told what to do.

One of the things that really makes you unique, and probably helps with your success rate, is the fact that there is no one way each person must do this.

A lot of this is psychological and you dig into each person's own issues. One person may need some kind of packaged diet regimen because that's what will give them the highest expectation of success. But, another person may need to eliminate certain types of foods entirely.

How do you determine which program is best for each of your clients?

Renée Jones: Everybody works differently. I do not give a diet at all because most of the people who come to me have been on some kind of diet before. I'll ask them how many diets have they tried and they'll list off eight or ten or twenty. So I don't give a diet because all diets do actually work if you follow them. Some work better for some people, but no diet will meet the needs of everybody.

I find that it's more of a transformational process. So what I do is I have basically four keys to weight management.

One is to know your body. You have to know what works for you. If I go on a high protein diet, I get kind of ratty and my husband just objects to that. So that doesn't work for me.

I know other people who can't do low fat, low whatever, low sugar, all of those. Everybody has something that works for them. So you have to know your body and what works for you and then do that.

You also have to know your emotional stuff. I know what sets me off toward an emotional eating binge. Most people do, but they don't know that they know it. I function like a flashlight to shine light when they're looking around for what works for them. They're looking around in the dark if they haven't paid attention to this before.

So I help them figure out what is triggering them and how they can fix that.

Then, you have to know yourself. Everyone is unique in what works for them. What motivates me doesn't motivate somebody else. Goals work in different ways for different people.

Some people need to be able to just do it themselves, with no outside interference or conviction about it. I do really well with helping other people meet their goals. But if I don't have some outside awareness from somebody else about what I'm doing, I'm more likely not to meet my own needs.

Some people don't need any structure whatsoever. Some are going to question every piece of structure. So you have to know yourself and what helps you reach your goal. What helps you create a good habit? What helps you break a bad habit? That's important to know.

And then the fourth thing is that you have to recognize this isn't a short-term fix. It didn't take me a week to gain twenty pounds. It took me a while. It also took me a little while to lose twenty pounds. It doesn't happen overnight. And once you get there, a lot of people say, oh, I'm off my diet now. Now I can have whatever I want.

Well, that's fine if you want to go back to where you were. But if you want to stay where you are, then it's important to find a way to maintain some of those really good habits. Recognize that sometimes you have to be an adult. Sometimes you know you have to eat your vegetables and not eat three chocolate sundaes.

One of the strengths you have is helping people recognize issues and recognize what causes them.

When people think, "I can eat whatever I want," it seems like you're able to shift that want, or at least shift the meaning behind that want, to a healthier alternative. You're helping them make better choices than what they had been making under their circumstances.

You're crystal clear with people about the existence of a magic bullet for weight management. You don't give easy answers. You give real answers, and that's so important and also speaks to your success.

What do you say to people that think that there is some kind of easy answer or magic bullet out there, but they just haven't found it yet?

Renée Jones: They already know what it is. The magic bullet is the power of their intention. If they want it and are willing to work for it, they can have it.

Some choices are just harder than others. I talk to my clients early on about this. When I'm talking about the different diets, I'll ask how many of you have taken those appetite suppressing pills. Several will raise their hands. Then I'll ask how many of you have found yourself standing in front of the pantry or the refrigerator looking longingly in? And they all had to again raise their hands.

You can deal with individual symptoms. You can take things that look after the actual biological need for food. But there's still that emotional tug because we're looking for something to meet a need other than hunger.

If you want a change, you can have it. But you have to want it, and you have to be willing to work for it, because, again, we're adults. Sometimes we have to work for what we want.

Sometimes people use that as a justification. They lean on that or some people just completely fool themselves. There are people that probably have the attitude "I don't need that ice cream. That ice cream needs me."

So many people try to approach this in a logical way, but you take logic out of it. You pretty much have understood that this isn't a logical exercise.

Renée Jones: No. It's never logical. They may say I want a thinner body, but they also really want that cookie.

Unfortunately, that cookie provides immediate satisfaction. They can have it right then.

Renée Jones: And that cookie does actually soothe them in the moment. But the problem with that, or if you've had a really rough week and you want an extra glass of wine or whatever, it does bring some relief. Then it brings that wrap-around guilt that feeds all of your issues over and over again.

I ate a cookie. I drank three glasses of wine. And then I had cake. And then I had this. And now I feel awful about myself, which only makes it worse.

That's the one thing people do and where you take logic out of it completely. If they are on a diet and by mid-morning they end up having a cookie or something, they say, "Well, I've already blown it today. I might as well just go ahead and binge the rest of the day and start tomorrow."

Renée Jones: Yes. But what if you say, "I had a cookie this morning. Okay. So the morning got messed up. But at lunchtime, I can get back on track, and I can save the day." Rather than, "Oh, now I'll have that big entrée at the restaurant, and then I'll have something else this afternoon and a big dinner tonight." Instead of a 200-calorie cookie that has blown your diet, you've added another 2,000 calories and you're in worse shape.

Whereas if you just say, that was not the wisest choice I ever made, but I can make a better choice next - then you have less to make up for.

That makes complete sense. You have obviously figured out a way to do that.

What led you to actually create a business around this that has allowed you to influence so many other people and to share this so successfully with others?

Renée Jones: For me, I think it was getting so frustrated with diet after diet. I tried them all. They all worked when I was on them, but then I would cheat. I'd gotten so accustomed to being on a diet that I was never not on one. So a little cheat here and there – I'll fix it next week or whatever.

Finally I thought I'm coming up on 50th birthday. Do I want to stay where I am or do I want to make some changes? And I decided I really want to make some changes.

My grandmother's family name was Broadway. We did our best to keep up with that moniker. The amount of food that we could pack away in a couple of days was just ridiculous. I thought that's not good for me. That's not good in any way, shape, matter, or form. I didn't want to end up at 60 still battling twenty pounds. Thank God it was only twenty pounds, it had been as many as 35. My family was fairly overweight, so I was the thin one at 145-150 pounds, which was really sad.

But figuring out where the cravings came from and what I was trying to stuff down and follow with a food chaser did actually help me. I finally got a little healthier emotionally, and that helped me make better choices for me. I started thinking about it in terms of not what looks good but what looks good for me, which helped me to stop doing the comfort thing as much.

A lot of times, it is trying to figure out what's behind that food. What is driving that behavior? If you figure that out then you can say, do I want to keep this habit? Or do I want to change this to something that's better for me?

You just described many typical families where overeating seems like an acceptable practice.

Renée Jones: If you lost weight, you were a traitor because you were showing up everybody else who said they wanted to lose weight. Serial dieters seldom actually lose anything.

This is just so profound, because so many people are affected by it. Going as deep as you do into the psychology of it has a tremendous effect on the people that you help.

Renée Jones: It does because if I'm not eating to comfort myself, then I'm saving a lot of calories. Because those comfort foods are highly caloric foods. Nobody comforts themselves with celery. They always comfort themselves with something that has a lot of calories, fat, sugar, or salt. The things that tend to, when put together, make it hard for us.

But once you unpack all of that baggage from your life, then you can make the choices that work for you. You can make those changes, because the baggage is driven by something you can't quite see. If we take all the baggage out and look at it properly, the keys to change become clear again.

At what point did you finally figure this out and put all the pieces of the puzzle together and have a map?

And what made you decide to come back over and share the map with others that are missing that piece or lost on that journey to find this? What drove you to decide you were going to help others with this and share this with others?

Renée Jones: My grandmother had passed away in September 2011. I realized I could eat myself to death because I really miss her, or I could take that energy and put it towards something that is good for me.

I had done all the diets, but I thought this could be helpful if I would just work on it. So in 2012, I started focusing on trying to lose some weight. It wasn't quick. It wasn't easy. It wasn't consistent, because it wasn't until October that I actually had lost those twenty pounds.

A lot of people hadn't seen me over the summer, for whatever reason, so they were like, "Wow, what happened to you?" And I started talking about the things that I had done and they said, "So you didn't just do a diet?" I told them no, because that doesn't work for me.

And as I talked to them, they asked if I would teach them how to do the same. And I thought, wow. This has got to be something different. It's not just a standard diet plan to follow. When someone asked me if I had a notebook, I said, no, I haven't created a notebook. Yet. This is just what I have done.

I recognized that a lot of people also suffered from the same kinds of frustrations that I had. I thought, "Well, good grief. If it's that helpful to my friends, maybe I should share this." And I was already doing some counseling and that sort of thing.

So I started focusing on the method, this is how I would counsel or coach you to meet your goal.

When you got the results that you get with the people that you were helping, that probably gave you the feedback you needed. It reinforced that, "Okay, I'm on to something here. This is working and this is really getting to the root of it."

Renée Jones: And it works for others. Once you figure that out with an issue that is this huge to women in general, and also to men, you can't keep that to yourself. That would just be kind of mean.

Your clients are certainly grateful that you are not keeping this to yourself and that you have shared this.

How can people find out more about Renée Jones and really dig into and realize and recognize these issues and find out what this is all about?

Renée Jones: My website is www.PackYourOwnBag.com and they can find information there about how to contact me. I'll talk to them by phone or in person, via Skype or FaceTime, whatever works best for them.

When you're ready to lose, I can help you win.

About Renée Jones

Renée Jones helps people lose weight—and any other baggage they're tired of dragging with them. As an ordained minister with a Masters degree in Marriage and Family Counseling and a Clinical Residency in Pastoral Care, she utilizes traditional and contemporary therapy models as well as relaxation therapy and horse assisted therapy. Renée has worked as a chaplain and counselor in long-term acute care hospitals and hospice for more than a decade serving patients, families, and staff. In 2011, she opened a private practice in counseling serving clients and colleagues in the U. S., United Kingdom, Canada, Germany, Romania, Australia, and New Zealand. She married a wonderful man named Michael in 1995.

WEBSITE: PackYourOwnBag.com

EMAIL: Renee@PackYourOwnBag.com

LOCATION: Arlington, TX

FACEBOOK: Facebook.com/PackYourOwnBag

LINKEDIN: LinkedIn.com/pub/Renee-Jones/23/b09/6a4

Helping the Helpers Transform Their Businesses

Ana Rosenberg is a Business Success Coach for those who help transform the lives of others with the good work they do.

Business people in the helping industries often struggle with building a successful, profitable business. They invest a lot of time and effort on mastering their craft, only to find out that talent is not enough.

In this interview, Ana shares how she helps modern experts who have a mission and a message figure out how to build that profitable business, while making a meaningful difference with their work.

Ana provides a lot of great marketing training and strategies to overcome the business issues that plague those who love to make a positive impact on the world.

Conversation with Ana Rosenberg

Successful people, such as people that are coaching or speaking from the stage, also have people that they turn to, to coach them in what they do.

What types of clients do you work with? What are the types of people that you are helping out there? What types of industries and businesses are they in?

Ana Rosenberg: What I would say is the common denominator of all my clients and all the people I help are people who are great at helping others get results and transform some aspect of their lives, whether it's their business, their health, their relationships, family relationships and their spirituality, or their motivation.

My clients range from coaches, therapists, trainers, authors, speakers, sports psychologists, consultants, all kinds of rising stars and thought leaders, and a lot of them actually are a combination of all those things. Some of them even have multiple talents.

For our conversation, it's irrelevant whether they call themselves coaches or seminar leaders. The important thing is they are great at helping people. They are really, really talented at doing that. They have this passion, this mission, and they know this is what they were born to do.

They invested a lot of time and a lot of effort on their craft to really be masters of the craft they have. But, sometimes they struggle with the profitable business part of the equation because they find that talent is not enough.

They usually think "I'm a great expert. People will see that and call me and book me." They live for a while in the Hollywood myth of people discovering their great talent.

However, at some point they realize that there's a 10% that is missing to be absolutely successful and to make their business a reality, because a business that is not profitable and sustainable is not real.

I love helping them because they are the most humble and the greatest people ever to work with. They are so passionate about helping others that it's really just helping them with that 10% that will make the difference in the success of their business. They already have everything else.

That's something that's so important and so common that people overlook. You see it over time in fields like medicine and therapy. You talk about how you work with sports psychologists, for example. I've seen it from chiropractors and other types of industries, where they are extremely good at what they do. They are so good at helping people.

But, being good at what you do doesn't necessarily mean that you are good at running a business doing that. I guess a good analogy is the cook that tries to open a restaurant. They may be great at cooking, but they may not be a great business person.

It seems like that's what you help people connect the dots with.

What are some of the big obstacles that you see with these people that are so good at helping others and helping motivate others? What do you see is preventing them from being successful in making this a business for themselves?

Ana Rosenberg: This has been my subject of study for years now. The first realization they have is talent is not enough. That's when they realize there is something missing. They also come to the conclusion of "Why should I know how to build a business? If I'm a dentist, why should I know how to build a practice?" Like other successful people, they are used to investing in finding the help they need.

The first thing that stops them from success is trying to speak an "alien language" to the perfect person they could be helping.

Let me explain this better. They are great at what they do, and they love what they do. Do you remember when we went to school and every teacher thought that their subject was the best thing on earth? The math teacher would say, "Ah, math is the thing."

So now you have this coach. Let's say coach in the sense of helping a person through a change, through a process that brings them to a result.

They start talking about coaching. They start talking about empowerment. They start talking about becoming the best person you can be.

Meanwhile the perfect person they could be helping is in front of them thinking "Oh, my God, I have this problem. If only could help me with this."

The only language they are able to hear and understand is the "language of solution to their problem".

This is what the coach should be saying instead "Oh, I have the solution to your problem."

As human beings, I'm sure we can all remember the time when we had a big problem that we couldn't figure out ourselves.

That is where we need to come from. From the insight of being human and having had at least once something we perceived as a big problem. That's the language we need to use in our marketing.

What is marketing? Marketing is a bad word for a lot of experts. It was a bad word for me for many years.

In fact, Marketing is the clear communication of value, in the language that the person that is suffering needs to hear, because it's the only language they can understand.

They want to hear a solution to their problem. That's it. That's the big thing. However, most coaches start talking about their modality instead.

The second thing is... I guess I'll be talking about all the "bad words". I already mentioned "marketing".

The next bad word is "sales". I understand why it's seen as bad because who wants to say, "Well, let me have a conversation with another human being who has a problem to see how much money I can squeeze out of them." Nobody, right?

I don't know anybody who would like to go to a business every day to see how they can trick people into buying their stuff so that they can get their money.

That's not how sales should be. It should be a human conversation in human language.

It's a conversation that starts much earlier than when a person picks up the phone and calls you. The conversation starts with you, with your "positioning".

What is positioning and how does it happen? As human beings, we very quickly assign new things and new people to "categories" or "compartments". We give them a place or "position" in our minds.

Oh, Joe. Joe is the Pizza guy because he makes the best pizza ever. And that is the "position" Joe gets in our mind. Whenever we want good pizza, Joe is the solution that pops up instantly.

The thing is to position yourself as the only solution to that person that you can help.

So when they call you, with all their suffering and all their insecurity – "I've been obsessed about this problem, it's a big thing and I haven't been able to solve it myself and I don't even have confidence right now that anybody can help me" – it's because they have already positioned you as the solution.

They call you because they think, "Ah, there is hope."

Everything else that they have seen and heard gives them the confidence to, at the very least, have a conversation with you.

Then, the only thing you need to have is a sense of direction for that conversation.

Another "bad word" for a lot of experts is "money". You'll know if you have "stuff" about money if you think "I don't want to ever talk to a human being about money." Overcoming that thinking about money is crucial to business success.

Let's talk about being human and having a human body and a human brain and how this play a part in the whole "marketing and sales process".

Sometimes we have a very visceral, real reaction in our bodies. You know the fight or flight response? All these chemicals flood our body...

Two common examples:

"I have to go do the presentation and everybody tells me to feel the fear and do it anyway."

"I want to have a conversation with a potential client but I am already feeling uncomfortable just thinking about it. I guess I'll just have to feel the fear and force myself to do it anyway".

No. What we have to do since we're in the 21st century is use the proven tools that science has given us to work with our human body and brain, and not against it.

This is something almost nobody talks about, but if somebody gets freaked out about money, about having a conversation with another person that can lead to a discussion about money, it's a real obstacle.

There are mind-body tools and techniques that help calm down the fear so you are able to do what you want to do.

Another factor that turned "sales" into a bad word is all the "sales training" that equals "sales" with "manipulation".

Selling has nothing to do with manipulating people, pushing people, giving people no option or putting them in a corner. We are not talking about saying "Buy this or your life will end."

The conversation started when they positioned you as the only solution to their problem. When they pick up the phone to talk to you or they have a meeting with you they will make a decision of whether to invest in themselves to solve this problem and get the transformation they want with your help.

By the way, the best clients for all of us experts are always successful people who are used to investing in themselves. They are successful because they are used to saying, "Okay, this is something that I don't know about. I give this person this bunch of printed paper because I know that that's the fastest way through the problem. They are going to help me get there faster and with less struggle."

That conversation doesn't finish when they give you the money. That conversation finishes, actually, when you help them through the process of transformation and they become fans of your work and recommend you to everybody they know.

That seems to be the thing that most people want to get to, because they're very confident in their ability to help. But you bring up such an important point about the sales and people's fear and distaste, their extreme view of what sales means to their business.

It seems that there are a lot of people that are really great at what they do, that almost do things to try to avoid sales. They think there are ways around having a sales conversation.

The fact is that you don't have a business unless a sale occurs. You help people get past, "You know what? If I do these other things, maybe I won't have to sell. Maybe people will just come to me and want to hire me. "

You talk about clients saying, "If I just get more education," or "If I get certified," or "If I do something to get better at what I'm already good at, that is what I need to do in order to get more business." That just doesn't happen, does it?

Ana Rosenberg: That's a Hollywood myth. Somebody will discover me because of my exceptional talent. We are going to the movies. The main character gets discovered. That's not how reality works most of the time.

Some of us have been to the "manipulation sales" courses, so it's not like we have fear of sales just because. We just cannot see ourselves doing that to the people we genuinely want to help.

Then, we have the Internet. The Internet hasn't helped. It has and it hasn't. It hasn't helped because it gives people the illusion that I can hide behind the website and people will click the button and hire me.

But for the expert, people need the conversation. They need to look you in the eye, even if it's an electronic eye, and know that not only can you help because you have the expertise, but you also care.

I know I get very passionate about this because you know what would be my dream? That nobody ever gets certified, goes to college or whatever, and leaves after making a significant investment of money and time and effort without knowing how to market their business, if they want to. That's what I would love to see happen. I think it is that important.

This is the ultimate freedom. We're in the 21st Century and some people feel they don't have that choice and that they have to go get a job because they're not able to have a conversation with a human being. That's crazy and this is the 21st century!

If we can get honest and look at it for a second, we'll see how important this is.

I'm a woman. I have been able to choose who to marry, what to study, what job to have or whether I start a business or whatever it is.

But most of my colleagues went to university with me and we graduated together. They chose the path of either freelancing (terrible) or, well, okay, "I'll go get a job that I don't want just because I cannot figure out how to make a living doing what I am great at".

I have no problem if you have a job and that's what you want to do. My problem is when you perceive that you have no other options. That's when I have a problem. When you want to do something different with your life. That's when I really care that you get what you want.

I'm not saying that you cannot come to a point when you can hire other people to do the sales part and whatever. What I am saying is that learning how to have a sales conversation is a big part of an expert business.

And I also like to use the words and call things the way they're called, and not use other words. I don't think it will help anybody to avoid saying that we have to market and we have to sell, particularly when marketing is just communication of value.

Our business depends on that. Everything else is optional and that's a big point. To get to do the work you love to do, you have to have clients to help. You have to be in business long enough to go on helping people.

So many people hit a point of frustration and start reconciling their feelings and start justifying their inaction.

One of the big ones I hear is, "I'm able to help so many people. I'm really good at what I do. And there are so many people that need my help. I should just help people for free because they need my help." They justify not having sales conversations because they use that as an excuse.

It really doesn't make sense for a business, but there are people that use that excuse. What do you say and do to help people that have come to that conclusion?

Ana Rosenberg: It's very common. Particularly, the more you like helping others. Well, I should give it all for free. At least I'm doing something good. What's the problem?

Leave the business perspective for a second and look at the person receiving that help. Usually, as human beings, we value what we invest in. You are positioning that human being to fail because that human being is not going to take your help seriously enough. It is not going to commit to the process and stay in the conversation.

What is missing there is the investment, and not only the investment of money, but the investment of time and effort. For instance, you buy two books. One is a $200 book, a rare edition. The other one is a $5 book about the same topic. Which one are you going to read first? The other one might even go unread.

How many of us download free stuff from the internet and never have a look at it? Because it's free - it's more or less saying it has no value. So, you are setting the person you are trying to help to fail.

From the business point of view, when you are beginning your business you are in no position to give everything away for free. But the more profitable and sustainable your business is then the more chances you'll have to help the people that really have no means to get your help.

In my business, I have a number of scholarships each year for young entrepreneurs from countries that really cannot afford my help. I could not have started there in my business.

I also could not start by sitting down and writing my life's work in an e-book and selling it for $20 because I would never be profitable. So that e-book, nobody's going to get to see it or buy it because I don't even have the means to finance the success of that thing. How many do I have to sell to make that a business? It's a very complicated thing.

But today, I'm writing a book and I'm happy if it helps just one person on the planet and my mission is fulfilled. Most people will buy it out of curiosity and will never even open it. It has golden nuggets inside. But today, I can say, "Okay, I'll take the time and I'll do that because I'm happy if it helps only the only one person that reads it. I'm in a different position."

Today I offer a completely free course in my website about how to start building and marketing a profitable, sustainable expert business to be proud of. I put a lot of solid information to get experts started and I'm also OK knowing that most people are not serious enough and won't even read it.

Another thing about "the money" is that some people are afraid that people are going to think they are "greedy". "What are they going to think of me? They are going to think that I only care about the money."

That is so true and people do have that issue. What you say is really powerful because you explain to your clients that if they give this information away, it's not just doing a disservice to themselves by not getting paid for their knowledge, but it's also doing a disservice to the people that are receiving the information, based on just the psychology and human nature of what they'll value.

When you do come across situations where people genuinely need your help, and they may not be able to afford the true value of it just because of perhaps the environment they're in, the only way you're able to get to a point to do that is by ensuring your success and selling your information first to the people that need and can afford it. Only then are you ready to really reach the people that desperately need it, but it would typically be beyond their reach. Is that right?

Ana Rosenberg: That's right. We all like to help.

But there is another point that is very seldom addressed and that is the person that is suffering and needs your help in whatever area it is. For that person who has tried other solutions, you have to be the leader. They have to be able to borrow your confidence to get through the problem.

So through your marketing, you are a leader. Through your sales conversation, you are also a leader.

When I started my first business, I would have conversations and then, when it came to the money part, I would start to twitch. They would be wondering what happened to this woman?

That's what I was talking about, the very real experience, like, "Oh, my God. I'm freaking out." What confidence am I giving the person about the value they are investing in? Is she sure or is she not sure? Is she going to be able to lead me through this problem?

The solution to this doesn't come from repeating, "Oh, I'm confident. I'm confident. I'm confident" or from positive thinking. It doesn't come from any of that.

It comes first from understanding the value of the result for that person, and taking it seriously so they see that you care enough to translate what you do into their language so they can understand you. They see that you are the person capable of leading them through.

It's a question of respect, too. It's a question of respect and also saying when applicable, "You know what? These are my recommendations. I'm not the person for you. This other person is the person that you should go to."

If necessary, if you're not the person, you should say that, too. It's not a question of trying to make everybody give you money for things that you're never going to help them. It's not a question of tricking them. It's not false confidence.

That's a very powerful thought that a lot of people don't consider when they are making those kinds of decisions. It's clear to why you're so successful at helping others become successful.

What led you to doing what you do? What led you to being a coach and helping the people that you help?

Ana Rosenberg: You know the person that loses a ton of weight, learns how to keep it off and then shows everybody how they did it successfully?

Well, I am that kind of business expert. I graduated from university. I was a language expert. Many, many years ago, I don't even want to remember how many years ago this was, I started my first business.

It was a coaching, training and consulting language business. Expertise was not the problem. I had to get clients. I was young and had no contacts. Nobody knew me in a very competitive market. But there was no option for me. I was going to make that business work.

I think of the beginnings of that first business as my "baby business". It was born weak and got sick. I was a determined mother. My baby had to survive.

Back then, there were not many baby business doctors. I was desperate. I was a desperate mother. Every single minute that I was not working with clients, I thought how am I going to figure this out? I was the person that went to all the sales seminars, the person that bought all the books.

Most of the answers I found in those trainings were things that I was just not ready to do. Kind of "there is no way that I will do all this. I'd rather starve."

So what was the solution to all this?

I kept what worked and threw away everything else. I got mentors. They are successful professionals that built successful businesses doing what they love, who by the way, happened to become my clients.

So I thought, "Oh, look at them. This is how they do things. Oh, this is the moment when they write the book. It's not here. It's there. It's here. Oh, okay. So this is how they market. Ah, okay."

And then I went and implemented this knowledge in my baby business. Then, my baby business started to grow. The fever went away. It started to eat again.

I got successful to the point that the first clients I wanted to work with were big corporations. So I became a consultant to big banks and corporations. I was not even close to the age of 30.

My competition thought, "Where did she come from?" And, by then, I thought it was normal. I thought every professional was doing what I was doing.

My colleagues said "How do you do it?" I come from a country with a terrible economy. Today up. Tomorrow down. "In any economy, you always have work. You have a name everybody knows. If you cannot do it, nobody else in the city can. How do you do this? Where does it come from?"

"Oh, come have a cup of tea with me or coffee or whatever you want. I'll show you what I've been doing."

From that cup of tea and coffee, that grew into, "Let's spend a weekend together. Let's have a look at how you're going to sell this;

how you're going to market this; how you're going to position your-self and your services as the only solution for the people who are supposed to work with you."

I cannot see that somebody that is talented cannot have a success-ful business, whatever the size of the business they want to have.

I'm not going to lead this conversation with the millions. As you have seen, I haven't mentioned the six figures or the seven figures or the eight figures and I won't. It's your decision what a successful business looks like to you.

What I'm talking about goes beyond that. I'm talking about feeling proud. I have a profitable business that I'm proud of. That's important to me. Also, the way I conduct my business is important. That's what makes me the happiest.

I went on with my language business for many, many years. I suc-cessfully sold that business. I went to China to work as a consultant and I built a private college in China from scratch, creating the whole marketing, the whole content, the whole thing.

But on the way to China, I met my German engineer husband. We dated. We had a long-distance relationship for many years. I didn't want to leave China. I was having a blast.

I moved to Germany to the middle of the countryside. There are more cows than people here. And what gave me the confidence to fi-nally say, "Yes, I can move and marry the person I want to marry and spend my life here is that I have the skills to build a business again, even in a country where I don't speak the language."

So that's the kind of freedom I'm talking about. I'm not talking about the "financial freedom" of "let's go to the beach and let's have margaritas on the beach." I'm not talking about that. Let's be real for a moment.

When somebody, another entrepreneur, another business owner looks at me in the eye, they know that I know what they are going through. And that has helped every single one of my clients.

I have never asked them ever to do something that I am not willing to do or done something like "let's trick people into buying this, pushing the red button instead of the yellow button".

Yes, but it's far beyond the dollars and cents signs. That's what most people are looking for and that's what most people consider to be true, true wealth.

Ana, how can someone find out more about you and your business and keep up with what you're doing?

Ana Rosenberg: Well, I do have a website and I have something more important than a website. I wrote a completely free course that is the substitute for coming and sitting down and having a cup of coffee with me.

"So where shall I start with all this? Even if I've been doing this for a while and I have clients here and there and I don't charge much and I charge per session, and I don't know how to structure the whole thing, where do I start? What should I not do? What should I stop doing?"

The first thing is to stop the overwhelm and stop the madness. If you go to my website, www.AnaRosenberg.com, you are going to find at the top where it says "Start Here." That's where you could start. It's the best substitute for a cup of coffee with me. I tell you all my secrets - what I have told all my friends for years.

About Ana Rosenberg

Ana Rosenberg – Creator of the Have It All Marketing System & Human Marketing – shows "Modern Experts With A Mission & A Message", especially Coaches, Trainers, Seminar Leaders, Authors, Speakers and Consultants, how to achieve what many of her clients describe as "business nirvana": having a profitable, sustainable business to be proud of while having a big impact in the world with their best work.

Recently recognized as a Top Professional in Business Success Coaching, international media such as NBC, CBS, ABC and Fox have cited her now famous quote: "Positioning yourself as the Authority in your field is the way to make competition disappear. There is no competition for an Authority."

Ana Rosenberg is honored to be ranked among the Top 10% of Social Media Users and counted as a Top Influential Coach, Speaker and Author by Twterland.

Ana is the Creator of the Have It All Marketing System, a step-by-step proven system to help "People Helping Experts" build a business to be proud of by marketing yourself and your business with ease and authenticity; communicating your value with confidence so that the perfect people for you say "Yes, I want that!"; attracting all the perfect clients you want and inspiring them to invest on the spot; and positioning yourself as the Authority in your field so that you get to enjoy your own version of a great lifestyle.

Ana provides cutting-edge business and marketing training via www.HaveItAllMarketing.com and www.AnaRosenberg.com as well as her social media Channels.

Ana lives with her dear German engineer husband in the German Alps and when they are not working, they enjoy travelling worldwide, cooking and sipping good wine.

WEBSITE: AnaRosenberg.com

EMAIL: Ana@AnaRosenberg.com

LOCATION: Weilheim, Germany

LINKEDIN: de.LinkedIn.com/in/AnaRosenberg

TWITTER: Twitter.com/AnaRosenberg

Arousal, Tension and Movement: The Formula for Real Communication in Your Business

If you had a team that included an anthropologist, a sociologist, and a psychologist all wrapped up in one person - that might describe Nicole "RapWithNic" Welch.

Nicole is a communications facilitator who helps successful business professionals overcome obstacles that are restricting the growth and profitability of their business.

Her unique background of having diverse life experiences have helped to shape her into a master of helping those who help others.

She excels in working with "techies" who focus primarily on sharing the nitty gritty and the ins and outs of what they are trying to market, much to the dismay of their unsuspecting prospects. After listening to several hours of a sales pitch, it's no wonder that more often than not, there is no sale.

Her many strategies teach this type of business person how to schedule their time, how to recognize when a sale is made and when to stop talking, as well as many other necessary life skills. Learning her strategies helps to improve both the business and personal aspects of their lives.

Conversation with Nicole "RapWithNic" Welch

It's remarkable the way that you are able to tune in and see peo-ple's issues in the realm of communication because communication does not always come through what people are saying, does it?

Nicole Welch: No. It usually doesn't come through what they're saying. That's what I usually try to help people with.

Communication breakdowns happen in business and relationships and in everything. Anyone out there that's an entrepreneur, and that has served clients, or that consults with people and businesses, knows how often that happens. And that's who you help.

You help people that are entrepreneurs, that are consultants, and that are extremely smart and gifted and talented in the tactical part of what they do, the techniques of what they do. But, like so many, they struggle in understanding what really communicates the value of what they do.

Nicole Welch: That's definitely true. I deal with a lot of analytical, left brained, very techie and tactical people. So they're all up in their head. I'll even tell them, "That's all up in your head here, so let's get down to some deeper root issues."

My client is the corporate guy or woman who is very successful. Maybe have lost some millions and gotten them back. Money is really just the commodity and the by-product here.

So what I'm going after is really just deep, deeper issues - deeper problem solving. Unpacking things for them so that they can see very clearly and take decisive steps and directions for where they're going.

When I say that they're good and they're talented at what they do, for the type of person you're dealing with, fulfilling is not their issue, am I correct?

Nicole Welch: Right.

The communication part is one of their big problems. It seems to me they finally come to a place where they recognize something isn't working in their business.

Chances are, even though they may not recognize it, it's probably not working in their personal life, as well, with these same issues. It carries over, doesn't it?

Nicole Welch: Absolutely. It definitely is carrying over. I always tell people, "If you're having an issue in one area of your life, it's likely that the theme of it, or the root of it is creeping under in other areas of your life – and it usually comes out sideways." I always use that analogy because people are just saying, "Well, if I have a problem, I know what it is. It's right there and I just deal with it and move on."

But, that's not really true because a lot of times, it's deeper than that. It's guttural or in the heart issue. So, I try to help these really techie, analytical, perfectionists. They're control freaks and they've had successes.

But, there's some part in them that just cannot communicate. They talk too much. There are too many facts and figures and too many things going on. So when they're trying to relate, they're finding that this isn't working. They get to a point where it's very, very urgent. There's a desperate need to change.

They're ready to change. They're ready to listen and be able to shift their paradigm to something that's a little bit more different and a little bit more out of the box for them to think and speak and understand people more clearly.

And really, it does carry over into their relationships.

One of the remarkable things is that you have corporations – big, multi-million dollar, billion-dollar corporations – that have the luxury of spending money when they're looking at marketing and when they're looking at selling their services. When they're looking at positioning themselves to the world, they hire companies that aren't just about writing copy or making pretty ads.

They are companies that have deep, deep roots in understanding, in psychology, in sociology. It's the whole basis of what focus groups are made up of, why people have focus groups, because of the psychological elements of this.

What you've been able to do is take those principles and put it within reach of that individual consultant, that individual self-employed entrepreneur.

When you come in and work with a client, generally they have too much. They're in that realm of "More, more, more. I have to tell people more about what it is I do." Is that right?

Nicole Welch: Yes. They have to complicate it and add more facts and details and data.

Your clients are not marketers in any way. What you do is simplify the very complicated world of the psychology of marketing by distilling it down to letting them know that their clients or their prospects don't want them to explain what they do. They just want them to do what they do.

Nicole Welch: Exactly. They want to know what the offer is. What's the hook? I use words like arousal and bringing tension into it. Just like you would in a story or your favorite movie, there's a hook. You're getting hooked in and there's an arousal happening.

So I basically cut out everything that they put in their marketing stuff or even their 30-second elevator pitch. I make them cut it down to like ninety words, and that's like killing them because they're dying. They feel they have to add more.

It goes back to the old features and benefits. They're always just rattling off what it is and they lead with their product and they think that's valuable.

I just reframe it to, "No. Let's look at you for a minute. Let's look at how you're speaking and how you're thinking and how you're feeling and how you understand your world."

As a sociologist, I look at the person in the context of the situation. We live in a society of norms and deviants and that's what you do. You look at it and you think, "Is that appropriate for this time? Is this inappropriate for this time?" That carries over in business, relationships and all areas of our life.

One of the things that struck me is your lack of judgment of what the situation is. It really is based on the circumstance. Like you were saying, "This is appropriate for this situation – it's not appropriate for that situation." It's not really a judgment because there are different parameters, depending on what's going on with the person and their prospect.

You mentioned three elements you use are arousal, tension, and movement. Those words are so strong, and you even indicated that using those can make clients uncomfortable.

It's so easy to recognize how powerful they are because you go into what those are and how those apply when you're moving someone from this analytic way that they're running their business, to the way that they should be, that's going to give them the most success.

Nicole Welch: Absolutely. Again, it goes back to framing. I use that word a lot because you pretty much are framing things in the context that they're being thrown at you or maybe you're entering into. So you're entering into a corporate oval table and there's no chair for you. What do you do?

To answer your question about arousal and tension and movement, I look at the biology of things, too. Looking at the movement of our society and even if you look at animals in the wild, there's movement there. That's what catches the attention.

When you're talking to an analytical person or a control person, they want to be in control of every move. And the word flexibility, I lived in a third world country in Honduras, Central America, and if you didn't understand movement and understand how to go with the flow and be flexible, you wouldn't survive over there because you never know what you're going to get and there was an element of risk.

That's what business is about. You just don't know what you're going to get over time. You don't know what you're going to get in your relationship. She could come home one day and say, "I'm out of here."

So there's movement constantly. I try to break an analytical of just staying in one place and have those people able to be flexible, start moving their arms, moving their body, start thinking about their feelings and seeing is their business going where they want it to go?

Because we live in an ever-changing society and we are constantly in movement. You hear terms like "stay in the flow," but if there's no movement in your business and your marketing, nobody's going to catch on to it. There's no hook. There's nothing there.

The analyticals are always leading with their product, and I tell them, "No, you've got to lead with desire." A lot of the business people do get this. Find out what they want and just give it to them.

But I go way deeper than that. Why don't you tap into what your desires are first, because you can't give what you don't have?

So, if you don't know what your own desires are and your own longings and what arouses you and it might not be the same thing as your client or your buyers or whatever, or even the person that you're in a relationship with, and if you're not in tune with your own, they're not awakened. They're not aroused by things anymore. They're so used to just seeing, and being inundated or consumed.

We're a consumer culture. We consume everything on a quick basis all the time. But, when you can't get in tune with your own desires, your own arousals, you won't be able to lead with that. You'll be a terrible business person, a terrible lover and a terrible marketer.

I really do a lot of work on pulling that out. It goes deeper than "What is it you want?" or "What is your master plan?" It's getting to the roots of those longings and what arouses you. What is it that all those senses, the five senses you have and then your sixth sense, your intuition - what is that drawing out of you and how are you carrying that over to other people?

There is a great quote that says, "Don't ask people what they want. Find out what it is that makes you come alive and go and give them that. Because that is what the world needs. They need life."

That's what arousal is. That's what desire is. I can walk into a room and because I'm in tune with my longings, my desires, and I know what they are (and some of them have been disappointing and some of them I haven't gotten to be fulfilled yet, but I know what they are. I own them and I validate them), I can bring energy and an atmosphere into a room and I can pull that out and awaken people.

When you can get your clients, and this is what I help my clients do, make something click, that's when you know you're digging into that arousal. I've had people actually come and tell me that their clients come in and say, "Man, what you just said, now that you communicated it this way, it clicked. I get it. "

I always use the term, "Do you get it? Does it make sense?" That's what arousal does. It's awakening so people do hear what's not being said and they do see the context of what's really going on.

You bring this down to a level on an individual basis and you're not changing what they do. You're not changing the way they do it. You're changing the way that it's perceived and its value.

When your clients come to you, it sounds like they're extremely rigid and you help them break that. Also, it sounds like once they start experiencing and digging deep, sometimes they like what they see.

They may be uncomfortable with what they see, but it's going to bring them closer to making them better at explaining their value.

There's a quote that says, "Necessity is the mother of invention." That's a very rigid way of thinking. It's the traditional way of thinking. Most people feel that, of course, necessity is the mother of invention. People need it. We create it. It fulfills that need.

But if you've looked at the last twenty years, the last thirty years, it's almost spun around now to where invention has become the mother of necessity, and it sounds like that's what you're creating with them.

Do you find they think the only way that they can demonstrate fulfilling a need is to give an information dump or all the details of what they do?

Nicole Welch: Right. I call it the tornadoes of unleashing information hell on people. It's overwhelming to the buyer, or it's overwhelming to the client. That's usually the complaint. My clients will say, "I just don't understand why. I told them. And I was there for six hours."

I'm thinking, oh, my God. I actually make them do a time budget. Because I have people who are literally researchers or analyticals. I actually had a rocket scientist as a client.

So I tell them we're going to cut to the chase and get to the root and reframe things and break some patterns, because patterns are ingrained in us. You have neuropathology, you can do behavior modifications, you can do your list, and do the tactics and the tactical things, but really, when it comes down to getting down to what's arousal, tension and movement in your life and in your gut, that is like where deep agreements have been made and deep truths and beliefs that are in your subconscious that come out in your business.

When I tell some clients, "Let's take the next executive step here and make some decisions," they'll say, "No, no, no. I need to finish talking."

So, I'm not changing their personality, but I am disrupting things and I'm making them look at that paradigm shift. Making them look at things through different lenses and having them come out with their own conclusions on reframing how they should speak and how they should think about their clients or feel about them and how they understand.

Really it comes down to understanding. It goes back to what I said, "You can't give what you don't have." So, you can't arouse your client or bring tension or urgency or movement into your business until you grapple with that yourself.

If you had to distill down what you do in a couple of words, it is that you connect the brain to the gut. People really understand that. They know that there are decisions and there are things that they do from their gut and there are decisions that maybe their gut is asleep and not telling them and they have to go to their brain, and sometimes they don't know which one to trust.

Are some of the people that you work with, and need your help the most, the ones that whose gut has been asleep or they've been ignoring their gut for so long and just going with the logical piece of it?

Nicole Welch: They definitely go with the logical piece of it, the self-protection piece. I use that word a lot: self-protecting. They do that in relationships. They'll do it in business agreements with joint ventures.

So, they're intellectually connected to what's going on - the facts, the data, and the information. But when it comes to tell me a story about this, any narrative or storytelling, how would you sell this or how would you pitch this, emotionally, they're not engaged. So the empathy level isn't really there.

I work on those eighteen inches from your brain to your gut, or your heart, or whatever it is you want to call it. Whatever it is when physiologically you're feeling those vibes or butterflies in your stomach. Or you're feeling like, "Oh, man, I just lost $2 million on this whole gig here."

It's really combining those. I do tell my clients a lot, "You're in your head. Let's go deeper. Let's go beneath what's really going on here, because those are just facts and figures. Tell me. Let's unpack that and really get to the root of the issue and determine how you can communicate this better."

It actually makes them better communicators because when they can unpack what they're been hiding behind or what they've been covering up, they can. We all hide behind facts and figures. "Oh, I've got a Masters degree and this and that." So what does that mean?

My tag line is "What you do comes out of who you really are." So again, I always go back to who are you? And what are you bringing? Because out of that, if you can get the "who" down, then the "what" just flows out, and it's fine.

It's not information overload. It's not you overwhelming your clients. It's natural. People are drawn to it. You're aroused. You're leading with desire and arousal, and you're bringing in those movements and maybe some tension, like, "Ooh, how do I get that? I want a second coffee date. I want to hear more."

It's really getting that hook into the other people. When I work with my clients, it's just trying to connect those with them. It's connecting that emotional engagement with the intellectual connections because the connections are there. They know how to do, how to innovate things and build things and create things, but communicating is a whole different ball game.

It seems like flexibility is probably one of the cornerstones of this, because it sounds like once they get that, then some of this other stuff falls into play. So let's take a look at a couple of scenarios so we can get a concrete idea of this.

If I'm a rigid person and you're saying that flexibility is the key, then the way that you frame it and the way that you position it is an asset. It's a virtue.

But if I'm thinking the way that a lot of folks think, flexibility - that means I have to be a pushover. That means I have to bend to other people's thoughts or ideas, when I know that I'm right or my way is the right way.

How do you reconcile the virtues and the benefits of flexibility with not wanting to be a pushover?

Nicole Welch: Good question. So when I'm talking with them about that, they will bring me the objections. "Well, no, I can't do that because blah, blah, blah."

These are the lines that I use. They're pretty powerful. I can again correlate flexibility to when I lived in Central America and worked with gang members. Diez y Ocho (18) and Mara Salvatrucha are the biggest gang members in America and in Central America. They are lethal. They are deadly.

I remember knowing I had to be flexible. We were literally living with these people. We were rescuing them out of the gangs at night in vans. Taking them out into some farm that was hours out of the city in Honduras. I remember thinking I've got to be flexible. I need to be thinking on my feet. I need to be a risk-taker, and I need to know that there are no guarantees in life.

The coolest thing was that when I was working with those people, and with the mentally ill, too, dealing with delusional, psychotic, I knew I had to be flexible because their intellectual connections aren't there. They're delusional. They're psychotic. They think you're the FBI and there are cameras in the ceiling, and, sometimes they don't understand the words you're using.

I would have to reframe the context of the situation and disarm them. Just disarm them with emotional engagement. Whether it was not making eye contact or maybe it was making eye contact, I really had to get in with my gut level and say, okay, how do I thrive in this situation?

That's what flexibility is for any businessperson and for anyone, whether they're analytical or not. You've got to be able to know is this true about the situation? Will I die if I don't make the merger, or if I don't give this guy the money, or if I don't decide to do business with this person?

You have to think on your feet. It's completely opposite of being a pushover. It's really being a badass. When you're flexible, you've got the highest commodity when it comes to that.

Now, I'm not saying this as far as time-framing. I think that's a completely different aspect, which I also teach my analytical clients to do. They have to be on a time budget and they have to frame themselves and that helps them. I frame it in a short amount of time, which also makes them more valuable, so they know you're not going to be talking to this guy for six hours. You've got twenty minutes. Get in there and get out. Talking about flexibility in those terms is a little bit different.

I'm talking about just getting away from your rigid self-protecting agenda and knowing if you're a risk taker. Are you going to die if you make this decision or not? Is this a bridge you're willing to die on? If it is, okay, we'll talk about that.

Or are you willing to calculate the risk and take it? And if you know a lot of techies and analyticals, they are risk takers but in a different kind of way.

You just completely rewired that idea of flexibility by framing it as being flexible is not being a pushover. Being flexible means you are in control.

You also made it crystal clear of why this bridges from business into personal relationships. Because so many people get into relationships thinking, "Well, it's not perfect now, but I think I can change them. I'm going to be rigid. I'm not changing, but I can change them."

You feel you're a pushover if you let them change you. But, by being flexible, you can accept the fact I'm not going to change them, but let me do what I do within the parameters that they live in.

Nicole Welch: Right. It goes back to breaking those co-dependencies, which a lot of analyticals have on their SOPs and their own lists and tactical ways. That's their co-dependency. I'm not okay unless I have my list or unless I have this.

In relationships, the flexibility is the one that has the freedom. I remember feeling so free in Honduras because I knew I could go with the flow. I could handle any situation that came to me. I could think on my feet. If I didn't, because it was such a relational community there, those gang members would have taken a bullet for me. I felt safer with them out in the streets, than I did with let's say the other workers we were with or the other humanitarian groups.

So that's the relationships. People get into relationships which are not flexible and they look at it like is it right or wrong?

If somebody goes into a relationship being very rigid and not flexible and they're in the mindset or the frame of this is right or wrong, that's where the non-judgmental stuff comes in.

I've been a therapist for years and you just stop. You don't judge. You hear the craziest stuff. A good therapist doesn't label anything right or wrong. I love those things in the mall when you go in and you're looking for a store and it says "You Are Here." That's what I tell clients. I say, "You are here."

Whatever the other person is doing or the business or the client or the relationship, if what they're doing is scary and it looks like you've got to lay the hammer down and be real rigid, you have freedom. You have choices. You have flexibility. You can choose. It's not right or wrong. It's just choosing what validates where you're at.

If people can get that, if they could really get that framework, it's about having choices. You've got freedom. You've got flexibility in the context of where you're at. That's Sociology 101.

Whatever you're doing, that's okay. I may have to put up some boundaries if it's disrespectful. I may have to say, "Hey, when you're calm we can talk later."

I always use that example of the mall directory, because you are here. Show up for life. What are you going to do? What are your choices? You've got freedom. You've got flexibility. You are not caged into a corner, and that's what rigid people think, "Well, no. I've got to control. I've got to self-protect." They do it in their relationships. They do it in their business.

You know what? People that don't label themselves as left-brained techies do it, too. We all actually do it. And when you can get the concept of how am I going to respond, not react, but how you're responding to the frame that you're entering into, the context of the situation, you've got it.

What afforded you the opportunity to gain this insight of experiences that most people have never, and would never want to, and may never be in a position to experience? What led you into this business - the coaching that you do and the consulting that you do?

Nicole Welch: Well, I reference Honduras a lot and it was one of those things where we got involved in some medical missions, and I have no medical background at all. We fell in love with some hearts down there in Honduras and we went back for a week and then we moved down there. I mean, literally, sold everything. My husband said we're going to go build houses. We never wanted to work with gang members.

I always hear people say, "Oh, yeah, I just fell into that," and I would never believe them. But I really did. Those doors of opportunity opened up for us. I did have an undergrad in criminal justice and I used to be a probation officer.

Studying the psychology of human behavior has always fascinated me and also how we deal with society and sociology. That actually changed my life forever. I think traveling to Australia, Columbia, we worked in different areas, I think really doing that and then living in Central America for years, I can say with 110% conviction, I will never be the same again because I did learn about risks.

Also, I did learn about thinking outside the box. I learned about money and relationships and flexibility and arousal and tension and conflict and wondering if you were going to get machete'd or shot. I kind of thrived on that.

I loved that adventure and I loved the fact that you cannot be attached to the outcome in your life. That's probably the one thing that I would tell anyone listening who is that analytical, who wants to be attached to the outcome. You can have goals and you can have things that you want to get to in your business or in your relationships. But there are no guarantees. There just aren't.

You can do the money back guarantee all you want. But in life, when you can accept the fact that it is an adventure and it's just full of risk and just realness and rawness, like what my podcast is about, it's like, man, when you can wrap your head around that and your heart around that and your gut around that, and really combine those things, you'll see those doors of opportunity opening. It's a freedom. It really is a freedom to people.

I worked in psychiatric doing social work and therapy for years, as well, which was a whole different ballgame. Working with people that are not intellectually connected because they're sick and they have some chemical imbalances or they're completely psychotic, I had to learn social dynamics really quickly.

I had to learn how to communicate with these people and disarm them and make them feel comfortable and make them feel not judged. Make them feel safe. Let them know that there was flexibility. Let them know that there was some arousal to getting better and taking their medicine.

It was kind of like it was ingrained in me. The experience, the encounters I had were on a very deep level. Probably almost so deep that I to this day can't really put into words how the experiences that I had in my life have changed me.

But again, it goes back to who you are. What you do comes out of who you are. It's made me who I am and I'm very aware of it.

I'm aware of bringing that gift to my clients and pulling that out of them. Awakening those things in them that they've been through - their experiences and their encounters so that they can benefit their clients.

I've seen it happen. I've seen them and their lives change. I mean change drastically, actually.

Your experiences allowed you to work in situations where flexibility determined whether you were right or not. Flexibility determined whether you lived or not, and so that would probably tend to create a little more flexibility.

When you are with gang members and people who could kill you and not think twice about it, then you might open yourself up to see things their way every now and then.

The real magic is the fact that you're able to take those experiences and then distill the elements that translate and apply to just about any situation or social dynamic or culture, and understand how those affect the outcome. That is so powerful, effective and valuable for the people that work with you and the outcomes that they get.

Very few people that have those experiences to be able to relate that and to be able to apply that to what other people are going through, so thank you for sharing this.

Nicole provides communication consulting to help you understand the psychology of relating on a deeper level with your market.

About Nicole "RapWithNic" Welch

Nicole has a Masters degree in Psychology. Her research has been published in the American Association of Criminal Justice Journal with her work with youth in Adult Prison. She has taught and presented at numerous conferences, workshops and seminars both within the U.S and abroad, and has mentored as a certified Life Coach for 3 years.

Nicole has started and operating several businesses and founded her own non-profit organization "Servant's Heart, Inc." Nicole and her husband lived in Honduras for 3 years and spear-headed several social justice projects including building homes, food programs, and starting and directing a Teen Challenge Center for ex-gang members.

In addition to consulting and speaking, Nicole is the Creator and Host of the Podcast show Real Time:Real Men Only. Nicole was a Mental Health Therapist in the Psychiatric fields for years and currently teaches Sociology at Florida Southern College in Lakeland, Florida, where she lives with her husband of 17 years and her two beautiful children.

WEBSITE: RapWithNic.com

EMAIL: RapWithNic@gmail.com

LOCATION: Lakeland, FL

FACEBOOK: Facebook.com/Nicole.Welch.5454

LINKEDIN: LinkedIn.com/pub/Nicole-Welch/40/814/714

PODCAST: Real Time: Real Men Only in I-Tunes

TWITTER: @rapwithnic

Coaching High Stakes Decision Makers

David C. Williams is a business coach to high stakes decision makers. He works with the most successful people in their industries.

You would think that these highly successful business people will continue to be successful - with no doubts or obstacles in their way. After all, they've already proven they can bring great ideas to fruition.

In this interview, Dave shares how he helps the ultra-successful business professional bring new ideas to market while working out the kinks their staff and personal relationships may have with leaving the status quo.

Conversation with David C. Williams

You've had the luxury of working with some of the most elite and successful entrepreneurs that are at the top of their game in their business. It seems like it would be an intimidating experience.

What's it like going in as an advisor to someone that's so successful?

Dave Williams: Well, you would think it is because, back from my military background, when I went into the Pentagon and got to meet all the stars [Generals and Admirals], I was really nervous. In the military, the people with the stars usually were the nicest people.

So fifteen years ago, when I got out of the military and got into business and was meeting the people that I've had the pleasure of meeting, I was a little bit shocked that these guys and women are the nicest, most generous people you've ever met.

They make you feel so comfortable the moment you walk in. All that television and misperception that goes on in today's culture is just wrong.

You have clients that I think average about 20+ years of experience in their market. They're successful. They're recognized industry experts that happen to be moving into a new area.

It seems that it would be very tough to advise them or say, "You should do this or you should do that." It also seems there would be a lot of resistance like, "Look at my track record. I know what I'm doing. Who are you to tell me?"

But, it sounds like it's almost the inverse. Do you find that your clients are open, or they probably got to that success because they are open to listening to suggestions or listening to experience from those that have been and have done what they want to do?

Dave Williams: Oh, you're absolutely right. In fact, it's amazing.

I've worked with people from my level, initially starting out, to some of the highest levels in the industries. The thing that I found out is that the higher you go, the more successful they are and the more they ask for help.

Not only the more they ask for help, but they make it really easy for you to help them. It's the exact opposite.

Plus, there's one thing I want to share with you. When you're working with them, they come up with these amazing visions and ideas and concepts. It's just such an honor to be in a room with them. It's almost like going to a Broadway play and seeing the best actors in the world controlling everything. It's just awesome!

From your vantage point, you're working with these successful folks. But they happen to not be successful, or have not had success, or are looking to move into a new market with success, and that's something that they may feel a little bit intimidated about themselves. They may be unsure or maybe they've had some stumbles as they're doing that.

So let's dig into what it is exactly that you get to help them achieve. It sounds like what you do is help them structure this and put together that and craft this.

It's almost like you play a role as not just a tactical advisor, but almost as a psychologist at this. There are a lot of emotional struggles that come along with this. It's not just about "Where do I put this," and the mechanics of it, is it?

Dave Williams: You're bringing up a lot of things that amazed me the most. Because of the success that these people had, you would think that they wouldn't have any fear, doubt or worries. That they wouldn't be like you and I, always having fear, doubt and worries that we deal with on a daily basis. But they are.

In fact, in a lot of cases, they have more fear, doubt and worry than we do because of the number of people that are depending on them to be successful. I like thinking of them as the old Maytag repairman. The loneliest person in the world. Or actually, the most successful person in the world.

The Maytag repairman is a great analogy. The product's so good, he never gets to get out and see people.

When you say that, it also makes people think back to the King of Rock and Roll, Elvis Presley. He was probably one of the most successful musicians and had so many people surrounding him. Yet, you hear about how lonely he was.

That's probably the case with a lot of your clients. They've been used to having these "yes" men around them for so many years. They've been used to having people agree with them because they've achieved success and nobody wants to rock the boat and everybody wants to stay.

But when they say, "Hey, let's do something new," it sounds like they might hit some resistance for the first time than they've experienced in a long time. I think that's where the psychology role probably comes in with you.

So what happens when someone has had great success for many years, and all of a sudden, they say, "Well, great, you know what? This is running smoothly. Now I want to move into this."? You would expect the people around would say, "Well, based on your track record, we're there. We're on."

But that doesn't seem to be the case. Talk about that because that's something that a lot of people may not realize. I can imagine it probably surprises your clients when this happens.

Dave Williams: Oh, absolutely. There is one thing I want to back up on a little bit.

Almost everybody I work with has amazing teams. And they're not "Yes, we agree with you." They're just very good in their market niche. They all bring up their roles and they're far from "yes" men or "yes" people. They're just really amazing elite teams.

But what happens, and you brought this up very succinctly, is that when their leader, who's already taken them to victory, is going off on a new battle, a new war or new mission, they really question what's going on.

In fact, one of my current clients is working with his existing partners who have stated, "Hey, it's time for us to get out. We're not ready to go on this next mission with you." And it was really quite a shock.

So when you do that, you would think - and almost all the clientele we work with do believe that when they announce this new mission because of their existing success - they're going to get parades down their home town street and everything else.

In reality, everyone - from their loved ones, their spouses, to their partners at work – questions, "Why are we going to go through all this mess, and sometimes embarrassment, of starting a new product in a new market?"

You brought something up that is also important - that it's not just their business associates. That's why I think you have tremendous insight into this. The fact that the people they work with, whether it's partners or their teams, and you talk about how incredible their teams are, they may have said, "You know, we did it. We won. Now, let's enjoy the success."

But they're ready to go and take on a new thing, almost like Michael Jordan. He won in basketball. Instead of just enjoying the success, he went on to play baseball.

And there are probably a lot of people that said, "Oh, no. I'm not jumping on this one."

But another left hook is they also have people in their personal lives, such as a spouse or other family member, that are not nearly as excited, and don't have the enthusiasm about this new venture.

What kind of toll does it take when someone finds out their relationships on the personal side aren't ready to take this journey with them, as well?

Dave Williams: Well, that's actually one of the biggest struggles they have to deal with. So, on their personal side, one of the things we start with is bringing clarity to their personal ambition, as well as their business ambition, as they're moving forward.

Because what we found is that if their personal ambition doesn't align with their business ambition, they're not going to be as successful as they plan. And as they're doing this, a lot of times they have trouble sharing what their personal ambition is with the people they love and care about most. This includes their spouses at home and their business partners.

It's about why it's so important for them to keep growing - because they feel they haven't achieved all that they can achieve yet. They haven't become the person they're supposed to become.

That is something so important for success that a lot of people don't think about. It goes back to just the tactical part.

So in order for you to be successful in helping them transition, you talk about how you make sure that things align. What is generally the response or reaction to them when you say, "Let's start here?" Or maybe they may have thought that we're going to start with "Let's get down to business" on the tactical side. Are they usually open to that or is that something that they may have a little resistance to?

Dave Williams: Well, let's take you through an actual example of one.

There was a project for medicine that we were doing that was going to allow the pediatric asthma patients in Southern California to be taken care of. We were working with a specialist, a pediatric asthma specialist.

He had to come up with this whole new way of taking care of people in their homes. A whole new triage system. Basically, to sign off on doing this for the first time, he had to put his career and his personal life at risk. Because in the medical profession, if you make a mistake, you're kind of done.

When we first talked to him about doing that, going through it, there had to be decisions made. I remember one was about using a stethoscope. Because you can't view a stethoscope through a television and look at it on video very well. You can't have him do it.

But he worked through it. His initial reaction was, "We can't do the project. I can't afford this risk." But then, after working through it and aligning his personal ambition with his career ambition of becoming a leader in telemedicine, he figured out a way to work around it and it became one of the most successful projects.

Let me share a result of what happened. So there was this one case of a 16-year-old boy who couldn't walk to the television to turn it on or turn it off without breathing hard. He had terrible asthma. He'd been clinically dead twice already in the hospital.

When we installed the system at his house, I'll never forget walking out with the case manager and the nurse. His mom walks to the door with us and asked, "How do I know what you just did will not kill my son?"

That's a tough question.

Dave Williams: Yeah. But I want to share the value. Because of the client, the specialist put his all into it and was totally convinced this would work. Six months later, that same 16-year-old boy had his driver's license, was in a marching band and was playing soccer. His life was changed forever.

That's remarkable. These decisions, like you said, they don't just affect your clients. The effects are far reaching, beyond what people even could consider.

You find out what their goals are, and if their goals are aligned, and if what they're trying to achieve aligns with both personal and professional ambitions.

What is it that you're helping them do to enter this new market now that they understand what the real challenge is and what the real work ahead of them is? What is it that you do when it's time to pull up the bootstraps and get going?

Dave Williams: The thing that we really help them out with first is to understand, when they're going after this new market, "What will make them happy to walk away from this deal."

Let's take another example.

One of the clients we're working with is very successful and he wants to do a joint venture with another business that's even much more successful. One of the things we helped him clarify first is "What will make you walk away from this deal?"

The reason that's so important is the smaller business, even though this guy is a very successful mid-sized business, when dealing with a joint venture with a much larger business that has the potential to change everything and take them to that next level, they focus only on how do I get that joint venture partner to sign.

We help them align not only how to achieve that result, but, going into those negotiations, what will be the result that you'll be happy to walk away with, with clarity. What will make you turn down this deal?

When they go into that negotiation with that clarity and that information, they're in such a better spot and the results turn out to be much better.

That is mind-boggling. When you explained that, it's impossible not to examine the things that really give you an insight into your level of commitment when you ask yourself that question.

It really is brilliant because so many people think about: "What will it take to get this deal? What am I willing to give up to get this deal? What am I willing to do to get this deal?"

But you have your clients measure their level of commitment to this by asking, "What will it take for you not to?" And that's when you start examining.

That's really fascinating how you do that. You said there is clarity that comes over people when asked that question. What have you seen when people are faced with and asked that question?

Dave Williams: I'd love to say to you that this happens in a fifteen minute phone call. But this usually goes on over several weeks. At first, they do it because they haven't thought about it. They really haven't thought about it. So it takes time to get a handle on the problem.

Then they actually have to come up with the realization, "Yes, there are limitations." There are reasons they would walk away from it.

Once they come to that realization, then we work on bringing clarity and specificity to those reasons, so they know exactly what they'll walk away from. Usually, the process actually takes a few weeks of working through to get to that point. But once they're there, it's like a different person.

In fact, we had one person, when she worked through this with herself and what she was doing in her business, she said, "I don't recognize myself anymore."

That's why Dave Williams is the name that people turn to when they're ready to do something like this. To be able to achieve that clarity is invaluable.

So let's talk about this. Once they have that clarity on what they're willing to walk away from, and when you realize that they see their level of commitment, and they realize, like you said, she said she didn't recognize herself, "I feel like a different person" - does that help them in either having tougher skin or being able to handle that lack of excitement or enthusiasm from their business partners, from their spouses or their personal relationships?

Because obviously, that's probably part of that mix, that level of commitment.

Is that part of when they overcome those obstacles?

Dave Williams: Well, it is. What we like to call it is they completely commit to their success. So once they have the clarity and everything, they start taking action. These actions they're going to take - it's not "no matter what the consequences" - but they're going to take these actions because if they don't take these actions, they're aware of the consequences if they don't take them.

We had one client on a government project. This lady was just awesome. It was a very high stress, multi-billion dollar project with a very short time frame, six months, to complete.

When we walked her through what she was willing to walk away from, what she made the decision on was that the government would not follow the existing regulations that were written, because if she did, it would guarantee the failure of her project.

To do this, she actually had to fire the leader of her team a couple of months into a six month project, and it had 30 different corporations involved. It's just amazing who these people become as far as leaders once they fully commit to their success and the actions they're willing to take and the results they can produce because of those actions.

Yes. That is extremely powerful.

Some people that may be hearing this and saying, "This is me. This is a position that I'm in. This is something that I'm about to let people know about this new direction I'm going. Up until this point, I thought that this was going to be so well-received." And, like you said, they're ready for the parade to happen, right?

So talk to these folks that are in this position now and kind of prep them for what they may be about to experience.

Begin with that popularity piece, where they think they're about to make this announcement and they think it's going to be confetti and strike up the band, but in reality, their partners, their loved ones, may not share the enthusiasm of what they're about to do?

Dave Williams: Well, I won't guarantee it, but it's almost a guarantee. And, it really comes down to human nature. None of us, me included... I love sitting in my chair right now. For me to get out and go dig a hole or do something that I don't want to, I'm going to fight it.

But one of the things I do want to share, a lot of your listeners are probably in a corporation, major corporations. One of our clients, who had taken his major corporation in a new direction about five years ago and produced about an additional million dollars in revenue, had another idea. Another direction to take. Another market to go after.

He was positive that his corporation would support him on this new direction. The way his corporation supported him was they said, "Great idea. You do it. Your expense. And once it's successful, then we'll buy into it."

So it's not only the mid-size companies. It's these huge corporations that have structures in place and cultures, that even when they've experienced the success, won't support them.

Steve Jobs was probably a perfect example of that back when he was pushed out of Apple. He thought his innovation would be fully supported, but they said, "You know what? This is a bit much for us."

Dave Williams: He's a perfect example and he got kicked out for twelve years before they realized their mistake.

Some corporations can realize their mistake quicker than that.

All right. So it's been established that it's probably not going to be the parade that they thought it was going to be with their partners, both business and personal.

You talked earlier that a lot of these people in these positions have really great teams. That these are people who are at the top of their game. They make the wheels spin in a business and they're really good.

But one of the most overused or common issues, especially with people that are CEOs or high level, is they like to use the word "just." All we have to do is "just" do this and "just" do that. I can tell from running businesses and from other people that I've talked to about running businesses, that that word "just" is very dangerous because sometimes they assume the abilities or the way things work are really a little bit different, even though their teams have a great record.

Talk about these expectations and how often they may not be consistent with what reality is with these teams.

Dave Williams: Sure. In fact, there's a lady in my mastermind who I think is just one of the most outstanding business people I've ever met and one of the greatest people in the world.

When she was leading a couple of multi-million dollar businesses, she came up with an idea for a third one, which was in a totally new direction and a totally new market. Her team rebelled. They said, "We can't do this. This is too risky."

She was talking in the mastermind of how, "Well, my team will love this. We've done two of them together. We'll *just* modify it."

Well, to make a long story short, she actually had to fire her existing team. Almost every member on it refused to go in the new direction because they thought that the new direction would harm the existing businesses.

A couple of years later, the existing businesses are doing better. Much better than they were. And now there's a third multi-million dollar business.

Do you see that it's both ways, though, that maybe the team over-reacted or misjudged the difficulty of coming on? How many times do your clients, do they maybe oversimplify? Or when they put the plan in their mind, it wasn't as complex as what it really turns out to be?

Dave Williams: That's human nature. We all say things are going to be easier.

That's where that "just" comes from. "Just" is such a dangerous word.

Dave Williams: In the military, we had a great saying, and it's still a great saying in the military, "No plan survives first contact with the enemy." It's the same thing in business. No business plan survives first contact with the market, the business market you're going after.

You have to change immediately and often. Actually, one of the qualities of a great leader is to be able to lead change. That's why I'm so privileged to work with all these great people.

One of the things a lot of people don't consider when taking on a new venture is how will shifting focus or taking on this new venture affect our currently successful business?

How do you see that? Is there a risk or consequences that are attached to their current success or their current business as they start moving to this new one? It's not just a pass/fail on the new one. It could be detrimental to their current business sometimes. Do you see them missing that? Or is that something that you have to take into consideration?

Dave Williams: I'm really glad you brought that up because I glossed over that point. The thing that's going on with almost every person is, "I'll 'just' have my team do these few extra things." Well, what they don't realize at the time is that their team's already fully engaged in producing their existing success.

Their team probably doesn't have the subject matter expertise necessary to produce the success in the new market anyway, nor do they have the time to do it. That's almost always one of the things that we always readjust after the planning phase, after we head out to market: increasing the team size and definitely bringing on new team members that have subject matter expertise in this new market. So I'm really glad you brought up that point.

They almost always overestimate the capabilities of their existing team, overestimate the time that they have to invest in this new market, and gravely underestimate the expertise and knowledge that they're going to need to be successful in the new market.

That's probably where a lot of the benefit of working with someone like you is – to be able to have the experience around that, but to be able to recognize where that's occurring. For a lot of people, success can be intoxicating. There are people that feel that success breeds success. To a point, that can be true.

How many of them can be a little bit overconfident that, "Well, I'm successful in this. Therefore, I'm going to be successful in that."?

What is it that they're usually missing or those things that everybody faces? How much of that do you see when you're coming in there, maybe just a little bit of overconfidence, even though they know that they need help, they need advice and they're coming to you? They may overlook that or just feel that they have a certain kind of a head start or a little bit more latitude because of their current success?

Dave Williams: Well, first let me share with you that I was the one that did it the most. I came out of my successful military career. I came out of a background where my parents were successful in business. I thought that I could take all my existing successes and accomplishments, go start a business, and just be successful.

Now, fortunately, that turned out to be true, but you don't want to know how many failures and bumps in the road, tears, late nights, and lack of sleep happened before I actually learned enough to be successful.

So I just want to bring that up to the guys and gals out there that are starting new businesses. That's one of the reasons that over 80% of new businesses fail within the first five years.

But more importantly to your point about the people that already ran successful businesses. They always believe - well, I'll just say the majority of the time believe - that they can be successful in a new market without getting any additional help. Let me give you a worst-case instance that I'm aware of which happened.

We had one client that we helped take to over a $10 million valuation in about twelve months. At that point, we recommended that to get to the next level, which was $20 million, we needed to bring in a new board and a new CEO and stuff. People who were competent because that would have taken him into a different market than they were currently in.

Unfortunately, the owner of the company decided that he could go into a new market without that new expertise, that new knowledge, and other things. After three years, that company was in bankruptcy.

So that's the negative of what can happen when people think their success can go into new markets. And I've already shared with you a lot of stories about the positive when they realize they can take their existing skills into a new market, as long as they supplement them with the necessary subject matter expertise and experience required for the new market.

You've exposed some pain points that people may have, that maybe they weren't ready for if they're about to announce this new venture that they're ready to go into a new direction.

A lot of times, that does take people by surprise. Obviously, the folks that are taking this into consideration and taking advantage of what you're saying today, they know that that may not be the case.

So maybe we can help them out a little bit in perhaps inoculating their board or their partners ahead of time, or at least to assess, maybe without going full-on with their announcement, to almost prepare them, so that when they work with someone like you, it would be a much easier transition or much easier onboarding process.

You talk about support from the board of directors. Support from partners. If someone before today thought, "Oh, this is going to be great. There are going to be cheers and hip-hip-hoorays." And now, they realize that's probably not going to happen. Rather than just unloading this news on people, what would you recommend that they do to perhaps inoculate them for what's about to come and make it easier to work with someone like you to do this?

Dave Williams: Well, this comes back to just doing the basics of what we were taught in Ranger School and other places in business, which is effective communication about what the mission actually is.

So this is a whole process and system and framework that we're talking about that needs to be put in place for any business. Actually, any business, any relationship, anything that you value in life.

What that means is, first of all, they have to work with everybody to make sure that they're working on the same mission. That they're aligned. This goes back to where we talked about getting the personal and business ambitions aligned. You need to do this for every team member, and that includes the board, to make sure everybody's aligned and moving in the right direction and gets the personal and professional benefit that they desire.

The second step in the process that we have is effective communication. You'd be amazed at how terrible people are at communicating with each other.

There are actually many ways you can learn to improve the effectiveness of communication for them by putting communication programs in place that allow people from all levels to be able to communicate effectively with their employees and with their peers. One of the great reports in Harvard Business Review a few months back was that 50% of all wasted time in corporations is because people are protecting themselves inside their own corporation.

What that means is they spend half of the wasted time worrying about how to protect themselves in their own business, in their own environment. It's just crazy when you think of it.

Then finally, after you've got the alignment, the vision and communications, the third step is to actually put together the plan, start executing and then rinse and repeat. Do it again and again and keep adjusting as each plan hits the market and it doesn't turn out the way you expected. Either better or worse.

Preparation probably makes a tremendous and dramatic difference in the rest of the journey.

Before we finish, what led you to find yourself in this position, to be working with successful people, the elite clients that you work with? How did you get from being in the military and working with the government, to where you are today where you have the opportunity and the respect and ear of people that are so successful, to helping them when they're ready to transition to something like this?

Dave Williams: It really goes back to what I wanted out of my life. For the first fifty years of my life, I only worked to achieve the next level of success, whether it was in school, becoming the captain of the basketball team or in the military, doing amazing projects and accomplishments. Or in my personal life or in my business life, as a serial entrepreneur and having multiple small businesses.

However, what I realized for this business was that I actually have the opportunity to design the life I want. Not just achieve the goals that other people had set out for me or recommended that I achieve, either from my family or the culture we exist in.

I reflected back when I was starting this business, about "How could I do things to design my life that would be better than what my parents had?" My parents are my heroes. My mom and dad, they're the American Dream, the success story. They risked everything to buy a grocery store in Bland, Missouri. Mortgaged everything out to the hilt to do it and then my dad was able to turn that into five businesses.

After a couple of decades of success, Walmart came in and put them out of business. One of the things that I wanted to do was to design my life and to help other people not experience Walmart coming in and killing their dreams.

What I want to share with you is Walmart did not kill my parents' dreams. Walmart was actually a huge opportunity and my mom actually shared this with me, I guess about ten years ago.

My dad and mom both realized that there was no way they could compete with Walmart, and there were many reasons behind that. But it was just an impossible way to compete. But what they could have done, upon that realization, was to recognize that Walmart was a tremendous opportunity. Remember, it was started in Arkansas, and Missouri is right next to it. Right above it, actually.

They could have sold their stores and invested in Walmart. Because they were better than that. And that's what my mom taught me. She said, "Dave, as you're doing it, remember, you're not fixed into your niche. You can design the life you want and move forward." And that's what I really wanted to do.

So in my career, I've been working with all these amazing people for twenty-plus years. They've been producing all these amazing accomplishments. I just decided it was time for me to design my life to intentionally continue working with these amazing people. Work with more of them, and work on more important projects to have a better life.

Truly amazing. It's just amazing to me how moments in time or pieces of our lives go on to make such a huge difference in their futures and other's futures.

Thank you so much for sharing this.

How can folks find out more about Dave Williams and what you're up to, and particularly if they find themselves in the position that they are about to head off into this new venture and to prepare for that, to get involved with what you're doing?

Dave Williams: The easiest way for them to find out is to go to the website, www.TheWCoachingGroup.com. That's where you'll find out a little bit about me.

But most importantly, I just want to share with people that are out there, being entrepreneurs and taking the risk and actually improving the world, accepting the bumps, the scars that go along with it, along with the rewards when they're successful, of how much I admire them for doing that.

It is my belief that entrepreneurs, successful business owners and people who will be successful business owners are the way to really significantly improve the world that we live in.

About David C. Williams

David C. Williams is the Founder and CEO of The W Coaching Group, Inc. With over 20 years of working with corporate and senior executives in various fields and businesses, Dave has a long track record of helping them succeed in their strategic initiatives, projects and profit goals.

An experienced business coach, small business owner, and serial entrepreneur, Dave has served as Founder, CEO, director and partner in numerous technology, product, and service companies and worked with startups to multibillion-dollar organizations.

Dave began learning the leadership skills necessary for business and entrepreneurial success during his 20-year career in the Army. Upon graduation from West Point, Airborne, and Ranger schools, he became one of the first Patriot commanders. During the last half of his military career, Dave won awards and was recognized for successfully leading and designing several technology projects (including telemed-icine) impacting billions of dollars.

WEBSITE: http://TheWCoachingGroup.com

EMAIL: ceo@TheWCoachingGroup.com

LOCATION: San Diego, CA

LINKEDIN: LinkedIn.com/in/DavidWilliamsCEO

FACEBOOK: Facebook.com/HighStakesDecisions

www.ingramcontent.com/pod-product-compliance
Lightning Source LLC
Chambersburg PA
CBHW061146040426
42445CB00013B/1580